Rand McNally POCKET ROAD ATLAS
United States / Canada / Mexico

Contents

Map Legend

══════	Toll ⎱ Multilane
══════	Free ⎰ Controlled Access
──────	Principal Through Highways
────────	Other Highways
•/ 35 \•	Accumulated mileage between red dots

- ⑤⑤ National Interstate Highways
- ⑥⓪ U.S. Highways
- ④⑨ State and Provincial Highways
- ⬛ Trans-Canada Highway
- ⑲ Mexican Highways

City Areas

✳ Capitals

0   100   200   300   400 **miles**

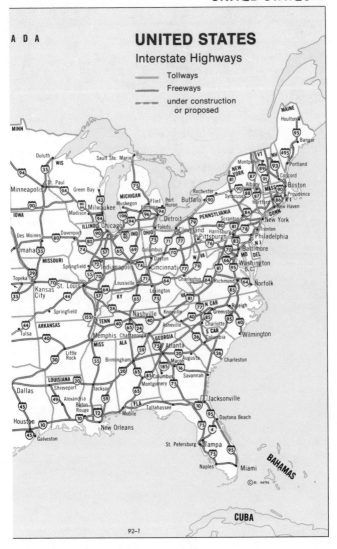

UNITED STATES

Interstate Highways

——	Tollways
——	Freeways
---	under construction or proposed

92–1

4/ALABAMA

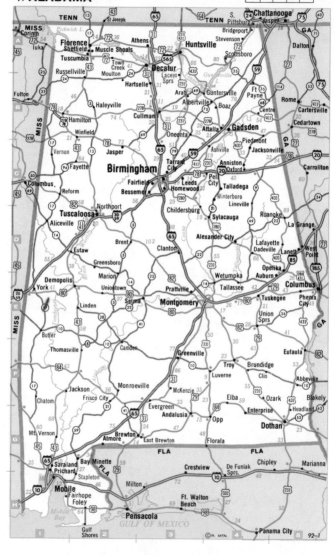

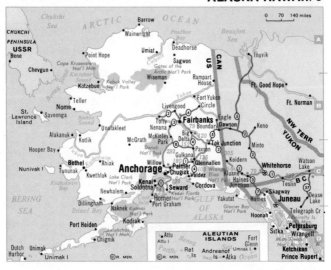

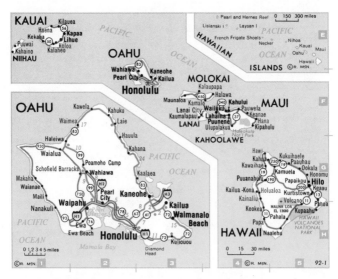

92-1

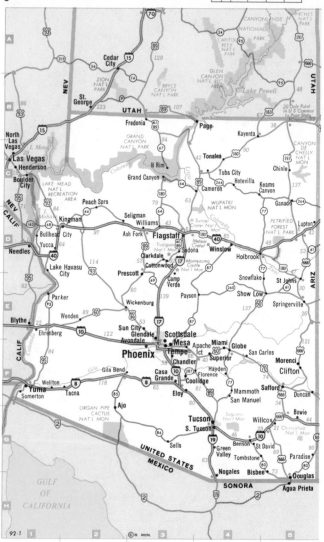

0 10 20   40   60   80   100 miles

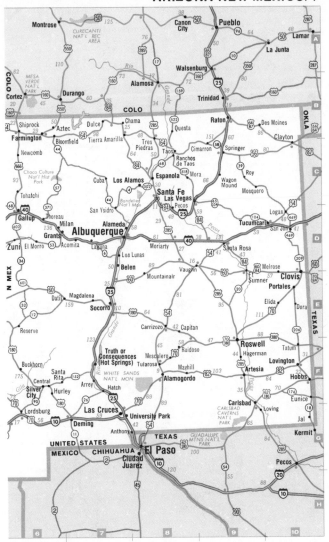

0   50   100 miles

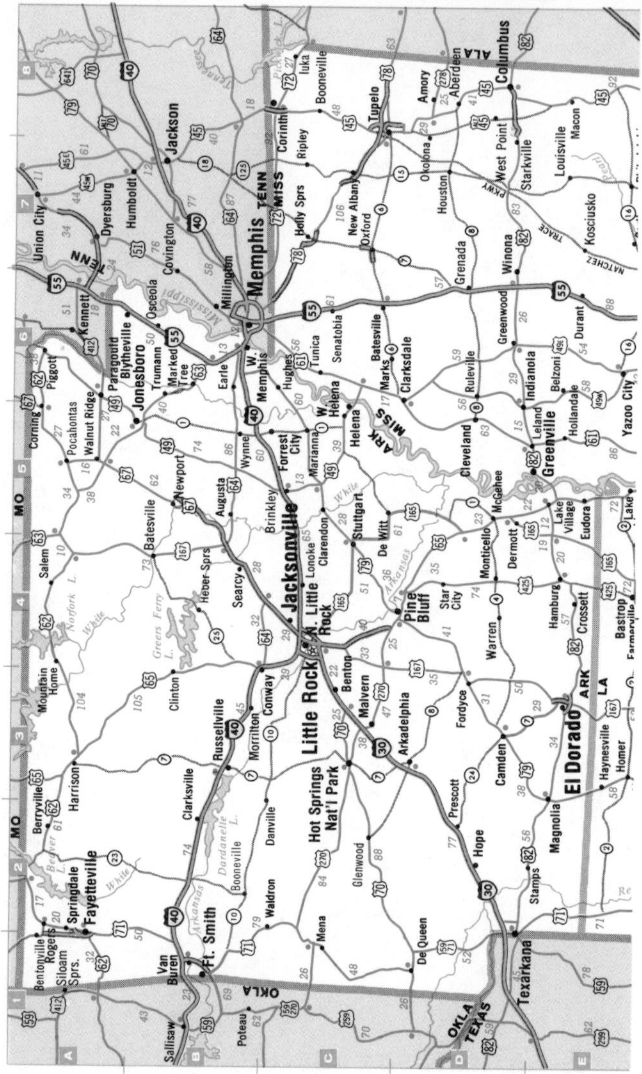

ALA
Columbus
Iuka
Booneville
Tupelo
Amory
Aberdeen
Corinth
Ripley
Jackson
Dyersburg
Humboldt
Covington
Millington
Memphis
TENN
MISS
Holly Sprs
New Albany
Oxford
Okolona
Houston
West Point
Starkville
Macon
Louisville
Kosciusko
NATCHEZ TRACE PKWY
Union City
Grenada
Winona
Greenwood
Greenville
Kennett
Blytheville
Osceola
Paragould
Jonesboro
Marked Tree
Trumann
W. Memphis
Tunica
Senatobia
Marks
Batesville
Clarksdale
Ruleville
Indianola
Belzoni
Yazoo City
Durant
Pigott
Walnut Ridge
Pocahontas
Corning
Earle
Hughes
W. Helena
Helena
Cleveland
Leland
Hollandale
McGehee
MISS
ARK
Newport
Augusta
Wynne
Forrest City
Marianna
Greenville
Lake Village
Eudora
Batesville
Salem
Heber Sprs
Searcy
Brinkley
Clarendon
De Witt
Stuttgart
Monticello
Dermott
Mountain Home
Clinton
Conway
Jacksonville
N. Little Rock
Lonoke
Pine Bluff
Star City
Warren
Hamburg
Crossett
Bastrop
Farmerville
MO
Norfork L.
Green Ferry L.
Berryville
Harrison
Russellville
Morrilton
Little Rock
Benton
Malvern
Fordyce
Camden
El Dorado
LA
Haynesville
Homer
Bentonville
Rogers
Springdale
Fayetteville
Siloam Sprs
Clarksville
Danville
Hot Springs Nat'l Park
Arkadelphia
Prescott
Hope
Magnolia
Stamps
Van Buren
Ft. Smith
Waldron
Booneville
Mena
Glenwood
De Queen
Texarkana
OKLA
Sallisaw
Poteau
ARK
TEXAS

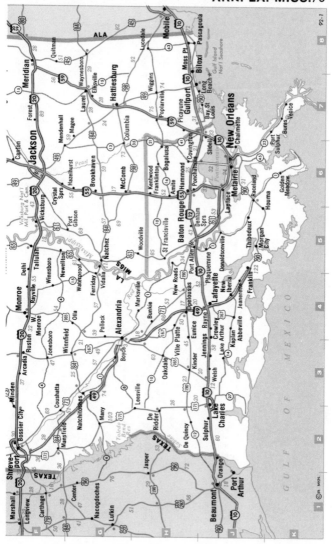

0 25 50 75 100 miles

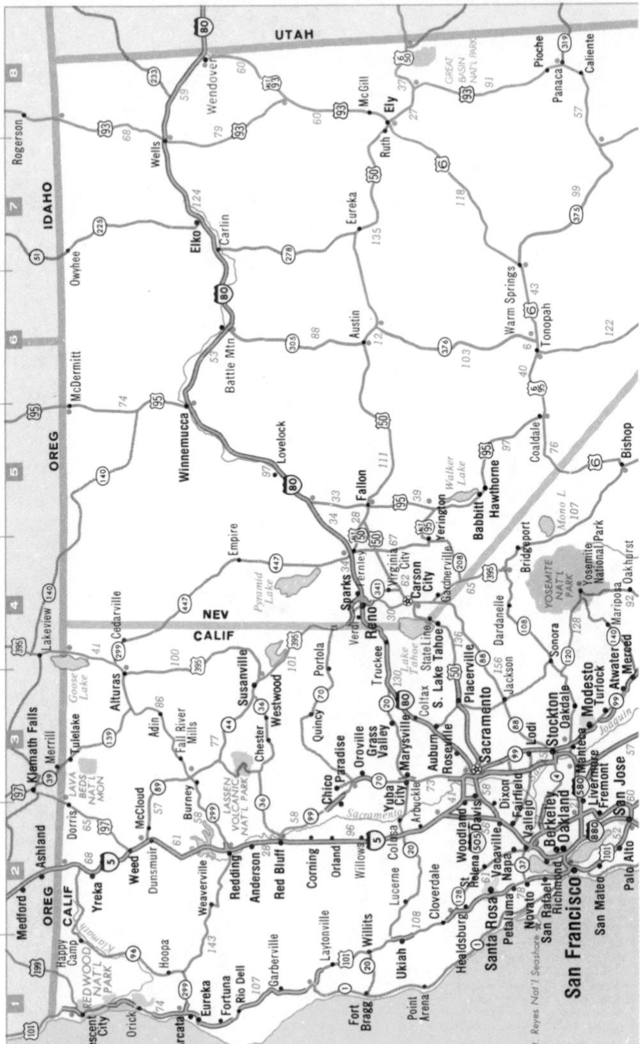

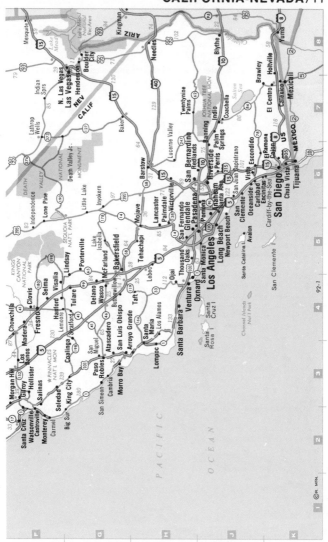

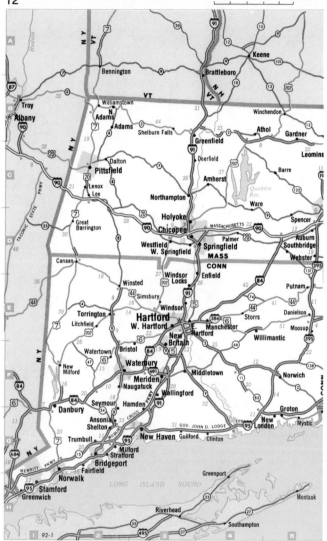

0   5   10   15   20   25 miles

0 10 20 30 40 50 miles

92-1

Map of Colorado showing major cities, highways, and surrounding states (NEBR, KANS, OKLA, N MEX, UTAH, WYO).

Selected labeled locations include: Imperial, Julesburg, Ovid, Holyoke, Sterling, Wray, Yuma, Akron, Idalia, Stratton, Goodland, Burlington, Cheyenne Wells, Eads, Holly, Syracuse, Lamar, Walsh, Campo, Springfield, Kim, Las Animas, La Junta, Ordway, Rocky Ford, Fowler, Pueblo, Walsenburg, Trinidad, Raton, Limon, Hugo, Flagler, Anton, Brush, Ft. Morgan, Greeley, Eaton, Brighton, Aurora, Denver, Englewood, Littleton, Lakewood, Castle Rock, Calhan, Fountain, Colorado Springs, Manitou Springs, Woodland Park, Canon City, Salida, Westcliffe, Great Sand Dunes Nat'l Mon, Fort Garland, San Luis, Alamosa, Antonito, Monte Vista, Del Norte, Center, Saguache, Gunnison, Crested Butte, Buena Vista, Fairplay, Leadville, Vail, Georgetown, Idaho Sprs, Boulder, Lafayette, Longmont, Loveland, Ft. Collins, Estes Park, Rocky Mountain Nat'l Park, Granby, Kremmling, Eagle, Glenwood Sprs, Aspen, Carbondale, Paonia, Delta, Montrose, Ouray, Silverton, Telluride, Cimarron, Black Canyon of the Gunnison Nat'l Mon, Curecanti Nat'l Rec Area, Dolores, Cortez, Mancos, Mesa Verde Nat'l Park, Durango, Pagosa Sprs, Steamboat Sprs, Oak Creek, Hayden, Craig, Meeker, Rifle, Palisade, Fruita, Grand Junction, Colorado Nat'l Mon, Naturita, Uravan, Dove Creek, Rangely, Dinosaur Nat'l Mon, Walden, Moab, Vernal, Flaming Gorge Nat'l Rec Area, Arches Nat'l Park, Canyonlands Park, Cheyenne.

Four Corners note: ONLY POINT IN U.S. COMMON TO FOUR STATE CORNERS

0 10 20 30 40 50 miles

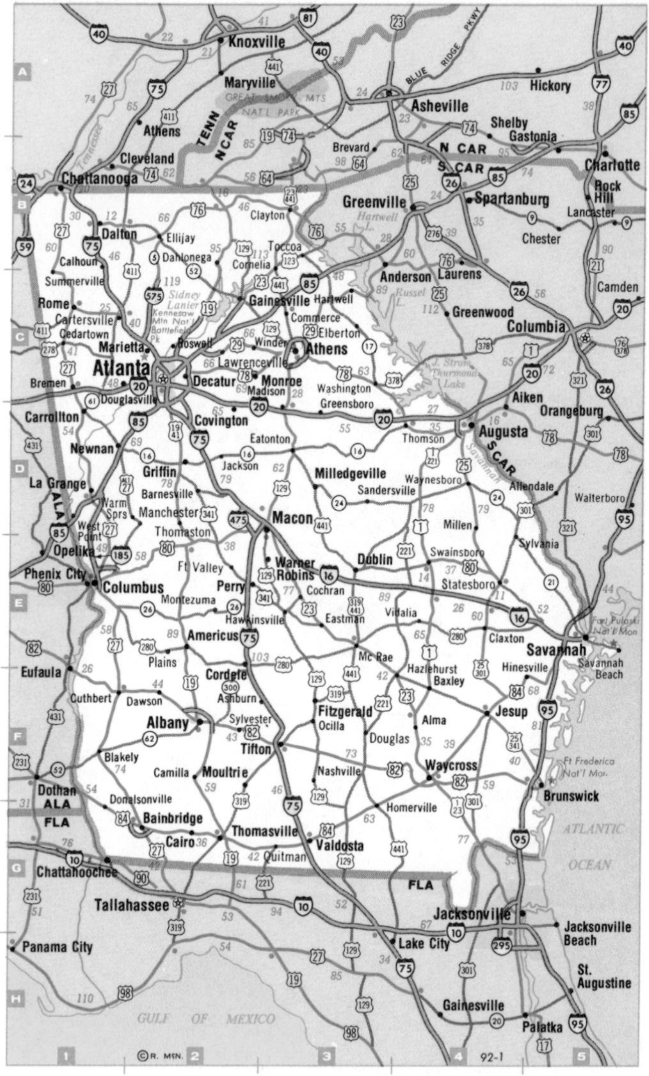

Map of Georgia showing cities, highways, and surrounding states including Tennessee, North Carolina, South Carolina, Alabama, and Florida.

Knoxville · Maryville · Athens · Cleveland · Chattanooga · Dalton · Calhoun · Summerville · Rome · Cartersville · Cedartown · Marietta · Roswell · Atlanta · Bremen · Douglasville · Decatur · Carrollton · Newnan · Covington · La Grange · Griffin · Barnesville · Manchester · Warm Sprs · West Point · Thomaston · Opelika · Phenix City · Columbus · Ft Valley · Montezuma · Perry · Macon · Warner Robins · Cochran · Eufaula · Americus · Plains · Hawkinsville · Eastman · Cuthbert · Dawson · Cordele · Ashburn · Albany · Sylvester · Fitzgerald · Ocilla · Dublin · Swainsboro · Statesboro · Vidalia · Claxton · McRae · Hazlehurst · Baxley · Alma · Douglas · Nashville · Waycross · Blakely · Camilla · Moultrie · Homerville · Brunswick · Dothan · Donalsonville · Bainbridge · Cairo · Thomasville · Valdosta · Jesup · Savannah · Savannah Beach · Hinesville · Chattahoochee · Tallahassee · Panama City · Quitman · Jacksonville · Lake City · Jacksonville Beach · Gainesville · St. Augustine · Palatka

Knoxville · Maryville · Asheville · Hickory · Shelby · Gastonia · Brevard · Greenville · Spartanburg · Charlotte · Rock Hill · Lancaster · Chester · Clayton · Toccoa · Cornelia · Anderson · Laurens · Greenwood · Columbia · Camden · Ellijay · Dahlonega · Gainesville · Hartwell · Elberton · Commerce · Winder · Athens · Lawrenceville · Monroe · Madison · Washington · Greensboro · Aiken · Orangeburg · Augusta · Thomson · Milledgeville · Sandersville · Waynesboro · Allendale · Walterboro · Jackson · Eatonton · Millen · Sylvania

TENN · N CAR · S CAR · GA · ALA · FLA · ATLANTIC OCEAN · GULF OF MEXICO

GREAT SMOKY MTS NAT'L PARK · BLUE RIDGE PKWY · Hartwell L. · Sidney Lanier L. · Kennesaw Mtn Nat'l Battlefield · Clark Hill Res. · J Strom Thurmond Lake · Russel L. · Ft Pulaski Nat'l Mon · Ft Frederica Nat'l Mon

R. MCN. · 92-1

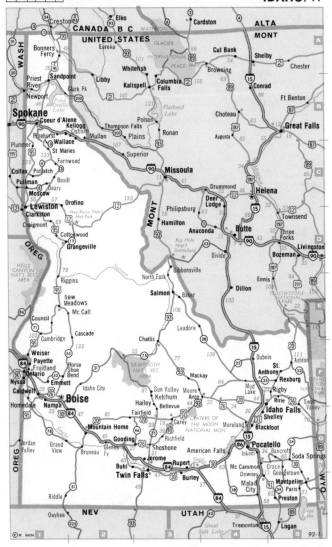

0 10 20 30 40 50 60 miles

92-1

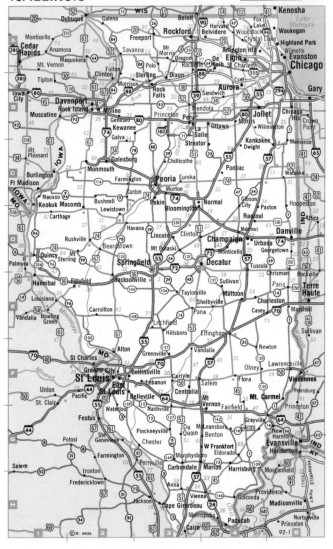

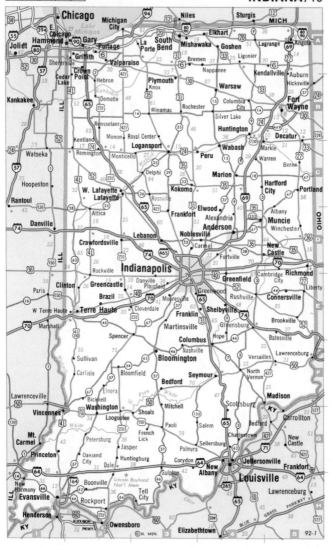

0 10 20 30 40 50 miles

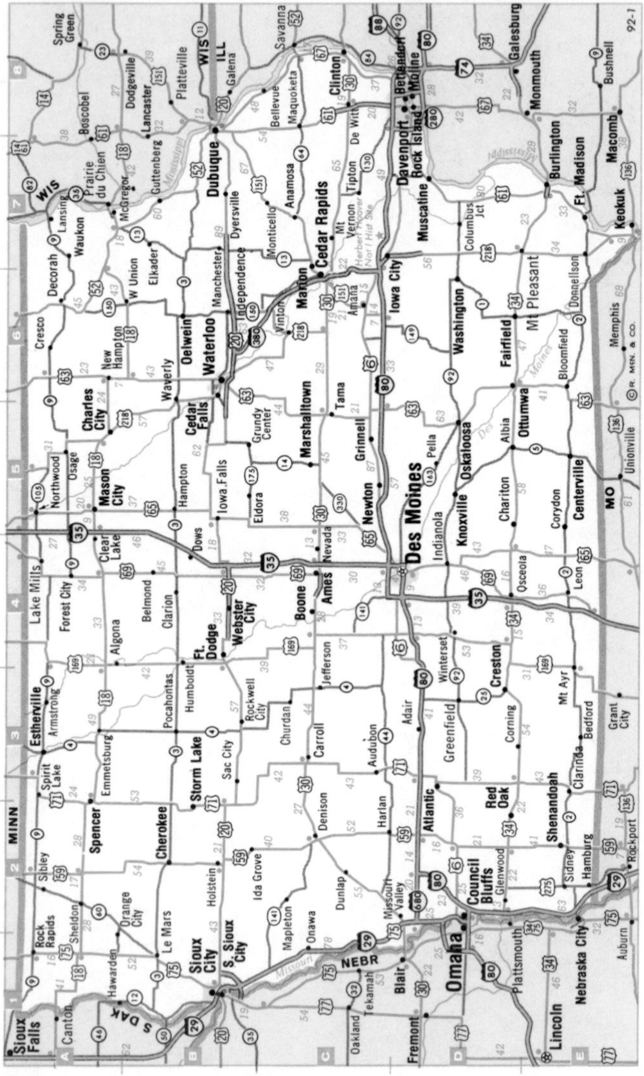

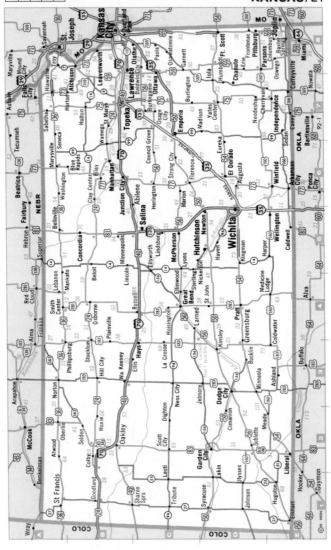

0 10 20 30 40 50 miles

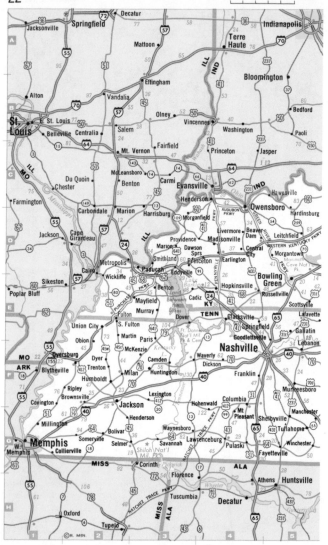

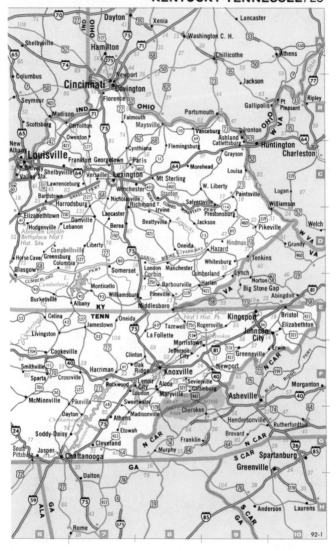

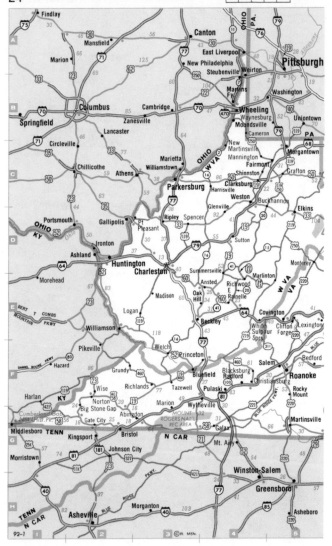

0 10 20 30 40 50 miles

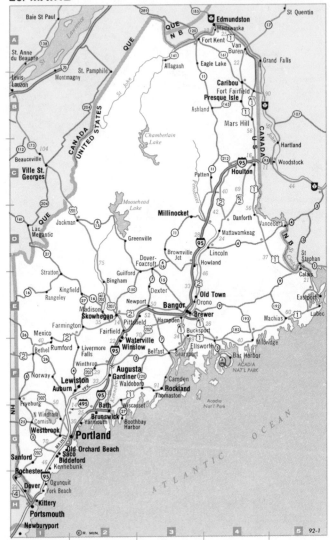

0 10 20 30 40 50 miles

Thunder Bay

ONT

Grand Portage

Grand Marais

Lake Superior

Little Marais

Winnipeg

Kenora

Keewatin

Sioux Narrows

Morris

Steinbach

MAN

Noyes

CANADA

UNITED STATES

Warroad

ONT

Hallock

Roseau

Baudette

Fort Frances

International Falls

Karlstad

Warren

Thief River Falls

Waskish

Big Falls

Voyageurs National Park

CAN US

Grand Forks

E. Grand Forks

Crookston

Red Lake

Blackduck

Marcell

Cook

Ely

Little Marais

Fosston

Bemidji

Cass Lake

Chisholm

Virginia

Eveleth

Silver Bay

Bagley

Hibbing

Fargo

Moorhead

Detroit Lakes

Walker

Grand Rapids

Hill City

Two Harbors

Lake Superior

Mahnomen

Park Rapids

Pine River

Floodwood

Cloquet

Duluth

Superior

WIS

Barnesville

Perham

Crosby

Moose Lake

Wahpeton

Pelican Rapids

Wadena

Staples

Brainerd

Sandstone

Hayward

Breckenridge

Fergus Falls

Onamia

Little Falls

Pine City

Spooner

Elbow Lake

Alexandria

Sauk Centre

Milaca

Rice Lake

Wheaton

Glenwood

Sauk Rapids

Cambridge

Browns Valley

Morris

Princeton

St. Cloud

Elk River

Anoka

St Croix Falls

Ortonville

Benson

Paynesville

Forest Lake

White Bear Lake

Chippewa Falls

Milbank

Appleton

Litchfield

Madison

Montevideo

Willmar

Hutchinson

Minneapolis

Bloomington

St. Paul

Eau Claire

Granite Falls

Glencoe

Shakopee

Hastings

Red Wing

Lake City

Wabasha

Marshall

Redwood Falls

Sleepy Eye

New Ulm

Le Sueur

St. Peter

Northfield

Faribault

Owatonna

Rochester

Winona

Tracy

Springfield

Mankato

Waseca

Pipestone

Windom

James

Amboy

Blue Earth

Blooming Prairie

Spring Valley

La Crescent

La Crosse

Luverne

Worthington

Jackson

Fairmont

Albert Lea

Austin

Spring Grove

Sioux Falls

Estherville

Spencer

Mason City

Charles City

Decorah

IOWA

S DAK

N DAK

92-1

©R. MᴺN.

0 10 20 30 40 50 miles

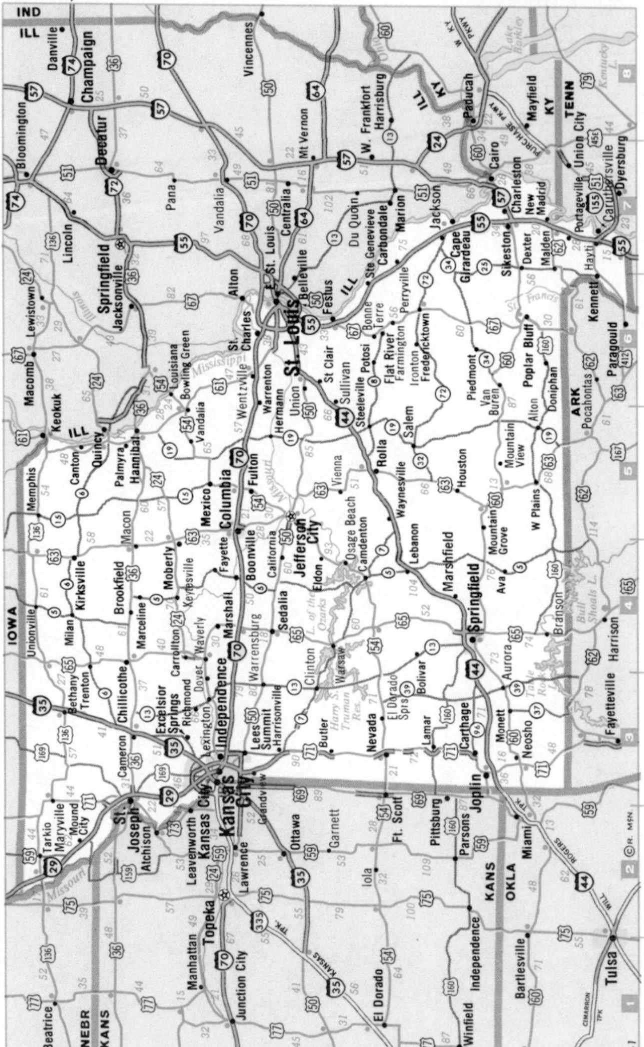

0 10 20 30 40 50 60 70 miles

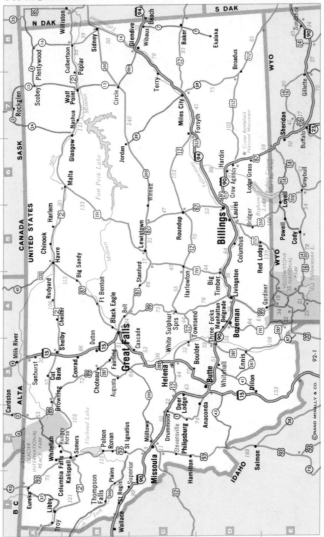

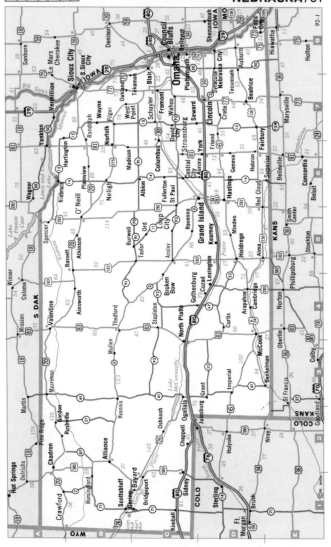

0 10 20 30 40 50 60 70 miles

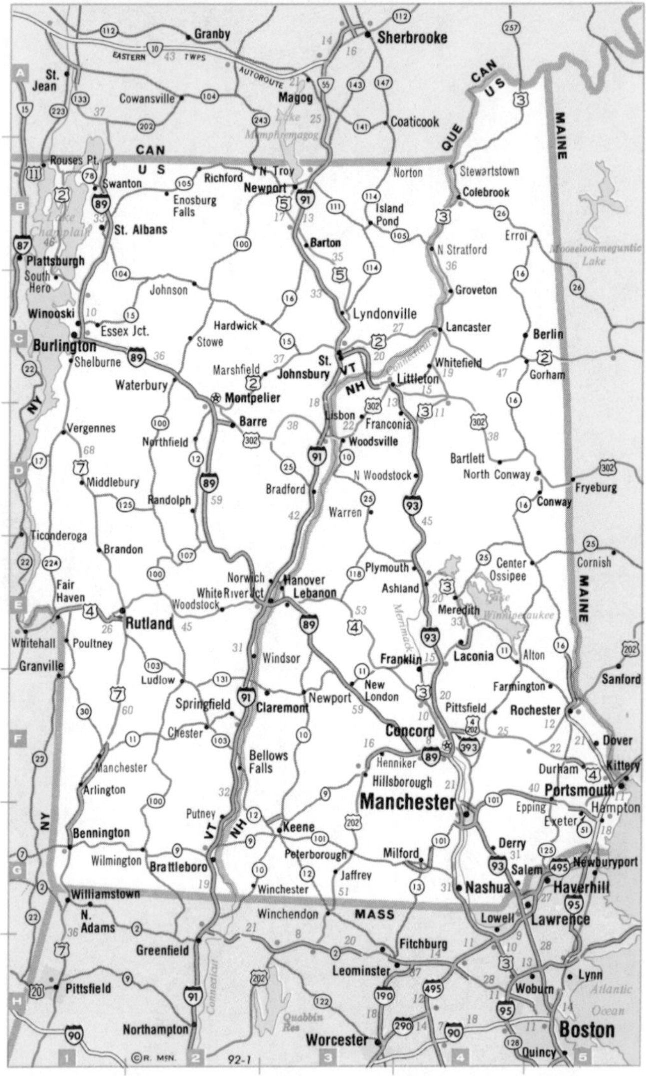

0 5 10 15 20 25 miles

DELAWARE
WATER GAP
NAT'L
RECREATIONAL
AREA

Peekskill

Colesville

N Y

PALISADES

Hamburg

Franklin

Oakland Waldwick

White Plains

Newton

Butler

Yonkers Paramus

Stroudsburg

Columbia

Netcong

Dover

Paterson

New Rochelle

Denville

Clifton

Passaic

Hackettstown

Morristown

Bloomfield

Newark Jersey City

Washington

Irvington

NEW YORK

Easton Phillipsburg

Bernardsville

Elizabeth

Bethlehem
Allentown

Linden

Bayonne

Frenchtown

Somerville

Plainfield

Flemington

New
Brunswick

Perth Amboy

Gateway Nat'l
Rec Area

Doylestown

Lambertville

Matawan

Red Bank
Eatontown

Princeton

Long Branch

Norristown

Hightstown

Asbury Park

Trenton

Freehold

Bordentown

Great
Adventure

Lakewood

Pt. Pleasant

W. Chester

Burlington

Lakehurst

Philadelphia

Willingboro

Toms River

Chester

Camden

Cherry Hill

Woodbury

Marlton

Wilmington

Woodstown

Glassboro

Manahawkin

Pennsville
Salem

Malaga

Hammonton

Ship Bottom

Buena

Egg Harbor
City

Vineland

Bridgeton

Mays Landing

Absecon

Millville

Pleasantville

Port Elizabeth

Tuckahoe

Atlantic City
Margate City
Ocean City

Smyrna

Delaware Bay

Dover

ATLANTIC

Cape May C.H.

Wildwood

Cape May

92-1

0 10 20 30miles

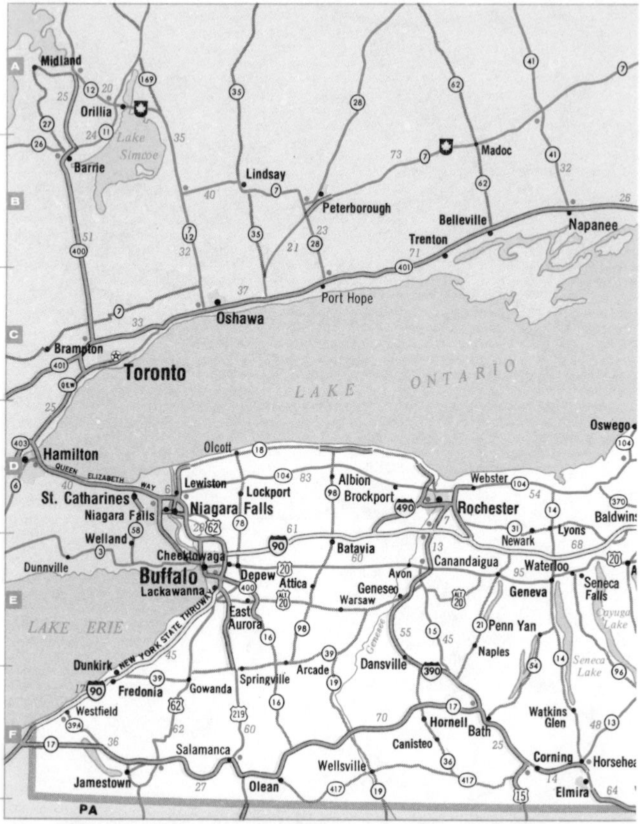

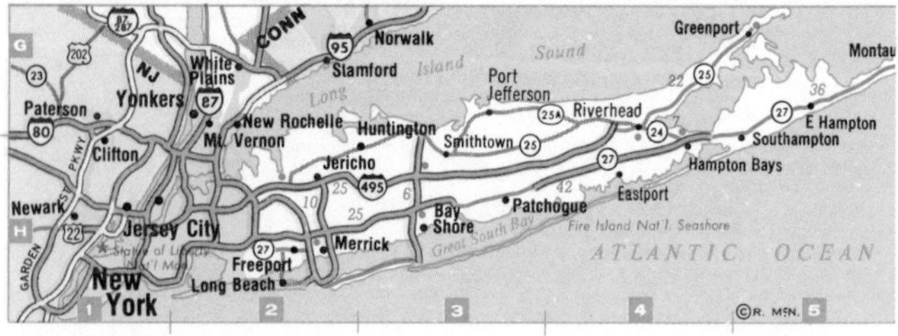

A
Midland
25
12 20
169
41
7
27
Orillia
24 11
35
62
Lake
Simcoe
35
7

B
Barrie
24
169
400
51
40
Lindsay
7
35
73
7
Madoc
41
32
62
28

Peterborough
23
28
Belleville
Napanee

21
Trenton
71

C
7
37
401
Port Hope
Oshawa

Brampton
Toronto
401
QEW

LAKE ONTARIO

25

D
Hamilton
403
QUEEN ELIZABETH WAY
Olcott
18
Oswego
104

Lewiston
104
83
Albion
Webster
104
54

St. Catharines
Lockport
98
Brockport
490
Rochester
14
Baldwin
370

Niagara Falls
Niagara Falls
62
78
61
Batavia
31
Newark
Lyons
68

Welland
58
90
60
13
Canandaigua
Waterloo
20

E
Dunnville
3
Cheektowaga
20
Avon
Geneva
Seneca
Falls

Buffalo
400
Depew
Attica
Geneseo
20
21
Penn Yan
Cayuga
Lake

Lackawanna
East
Aurora
16
98
Warsaw
55
15
45
Naples
54
14
96

LAKE ERIE
39
Springville
Arcade
19
Dansville
390
Seneca
Lake

Dunkirk
90
39
45
Gowanda
14
70
17
Hornell
Bath
Watkins
Glen
48
13

Fredonia
62
219
60
Canisteo
36
25
Corning
Horsehea

Westfield
394
Salamanca
Wellsville
417
19
417
14
Elmira
15
64

F
17
36
27
Jamestown
Olean

PA

G
76
202
Norwalk
95
Greenport
Montau

23
White
Plains
Stamford
LONG Island Sound
25
36

Paterson
Yonkers
87
Port
Jefferson
Riverhead
24
25

80
Clifton
New Rochelle
Mt. Vernon
Huntington
234
Smithtown
25
27
Southampton
E Hampton

Jericho
495
6
Hampton Bays

H
Newark
Jersey City
10
25
Patchogue
Eastport

122
GARDEN STATE PKWY
27
Merrick
Bay
Shore
Fire Island Nat'l Seashore

New
York
Freeport
Long Beach
Great South Bay
ATLANTIC OCEAN

NJ
CONN

Statue of Liberty

© R. M♭N.

1   **2**   **3**   **4**   **5**

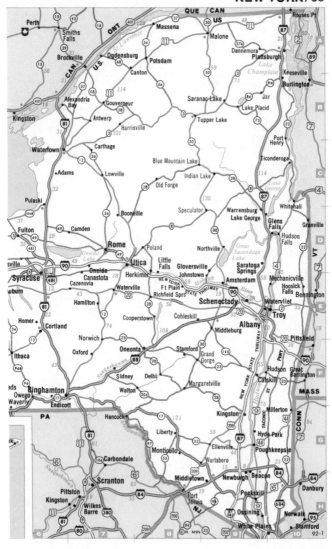

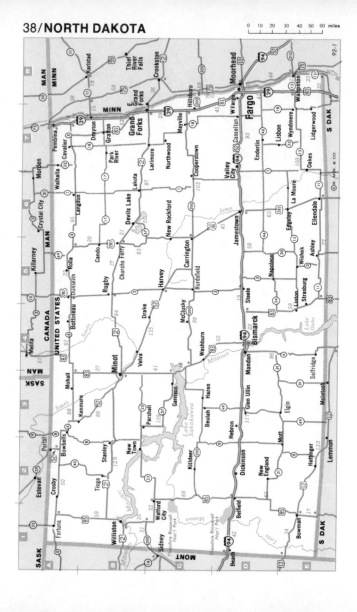

0 10 20 30 40 50 60 70 miles

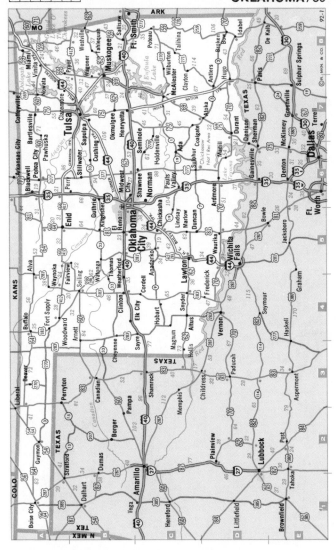

0 5 10 20 30 miles

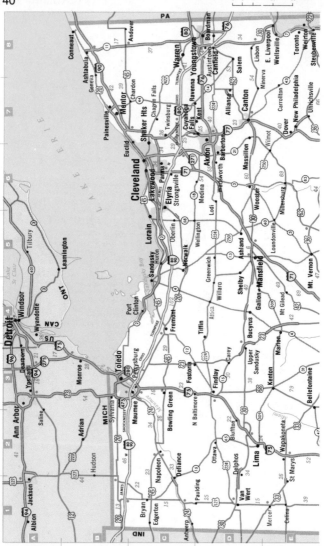

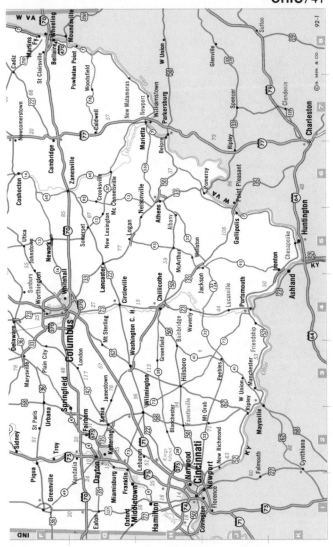

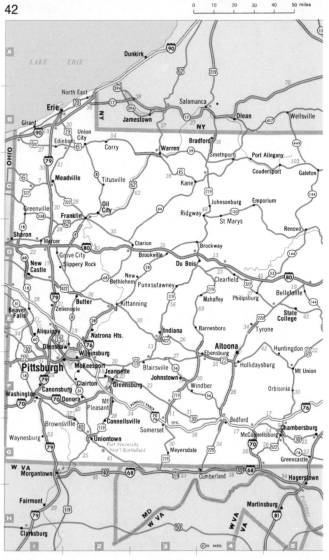

0   10   20   30   40   50 miles

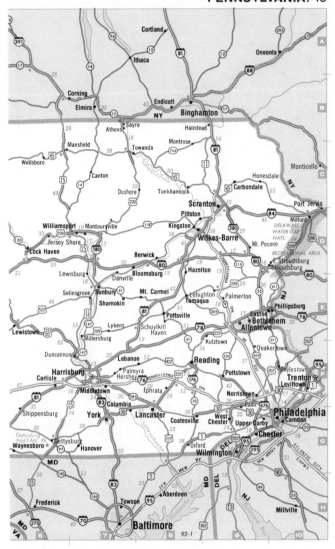

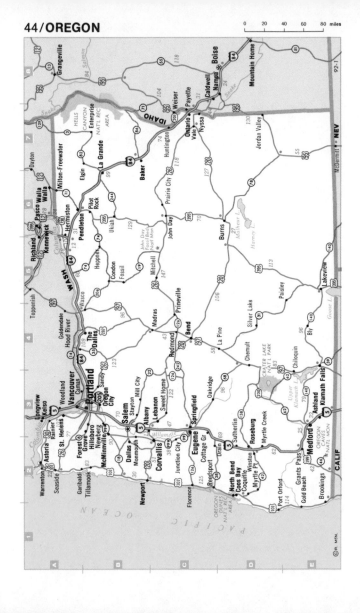

0 10 20 30 40 50 60 miles

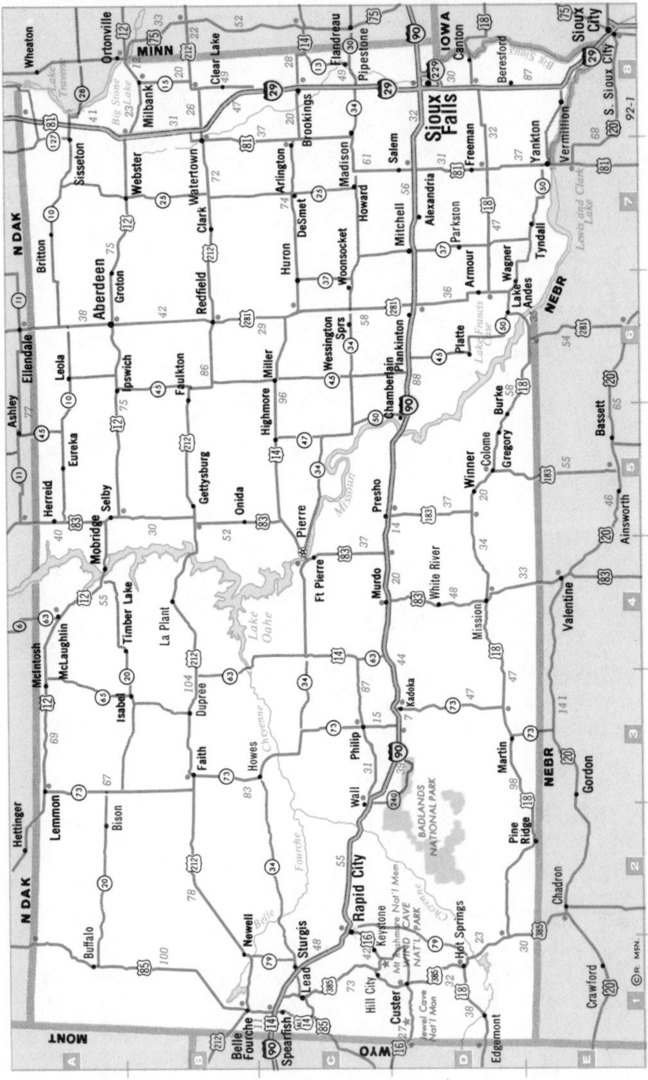

Wheaton

Ortonville
MINN
Clear Lake
Flandreau
Pipestone
IOWA
Sioux City
Canton
S. Sioux City

Milbank
Big Stone Lake
Clark
Watertown
Brookings
Sioux Falls
Beresford
92-1

Sisseton
Webster
Arlington
Madison
Salem
Yankton
Vermillion

N DAK
Britton
Aberdeen
Groton
Redfield
Huron
DeSmet
Howard
Mitchell
Alexandria
Parkston
Freeman
Tyndall

Ellendale
Leola
Ipswich
Faulkton
Miller
Woonsocket
Armour
Wagner
Lake Andes

Ashley
Eureka
Gettysburg
Highmore
Wessington Sprs
Wessington
Pukwana
Chamberlain
Platte
Burke

Herreid
Selby
Onida
Pierre
Presho
Winner
Colome
Gregory

NEBR

Mobridge
Ft Pierre
Murdo
White River
Mission

Timber Lake
La Plant
Dupree
Kadoka
Martin

McIntosh
McLaughlin
Isabel
Howes
Philip
Wall

Lemmon
Bison
Faith
BADLANDS NATIONAL PARK
Pine Ridge

Hettinger
Buffalo
Newell
Rapid City
Sturgis
Lead
Keystone
Hot Springs
Chadron

N DAK
Belle Fourche
Spearfish
WIND CAVE NAT'L PARK
Custer
Hill City
Edgemont
Crawford

WYO
MONT

Lake Oahe
Lake Francis Case
Lewis and Clark Lake
Missouri River
Cheyenne River
Belle Fourche

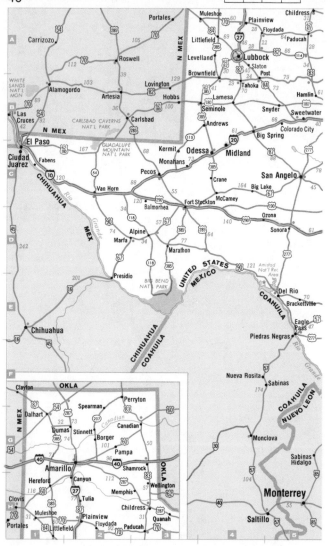

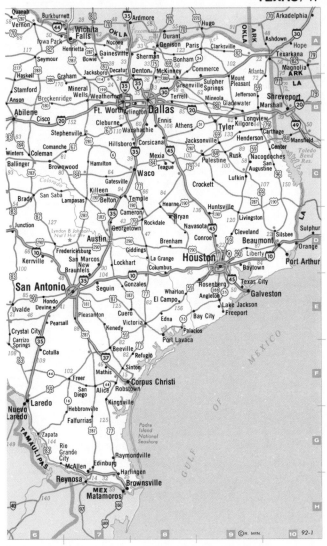

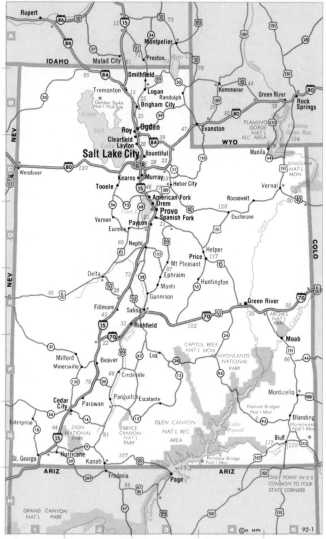

0 10 20 30 40 50 miles

92-1

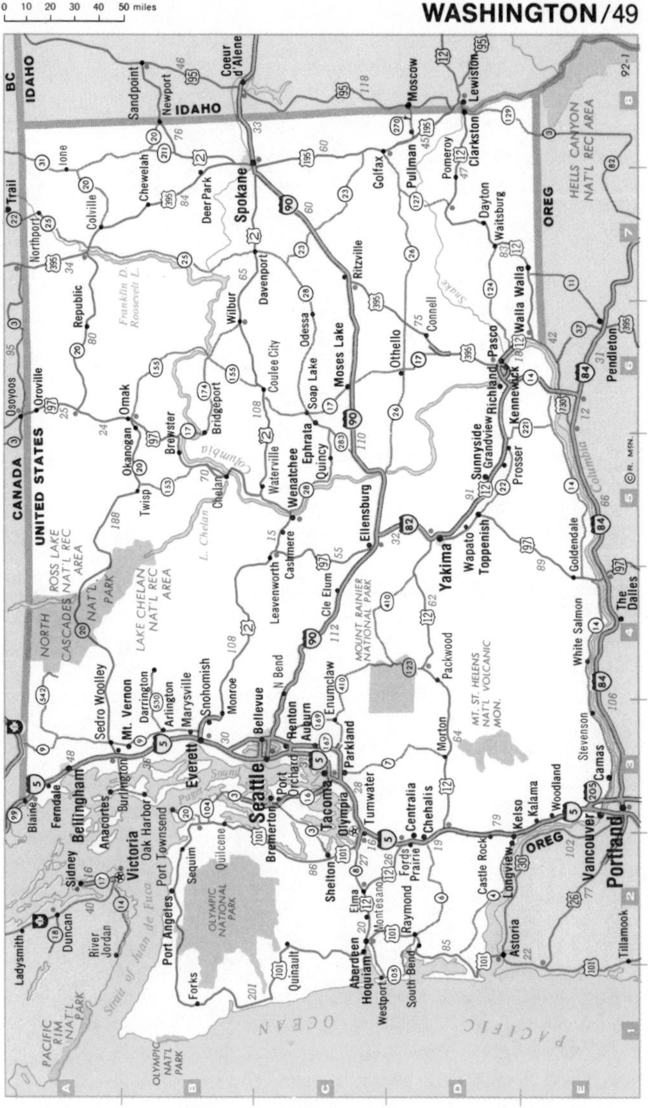

0 10 20 30 40 50 miles

Road map of Washington State

0 10 20 30 40 50 60 miles

Rainy Lake

ONT
MINN
Voyageurs National Park

CAN
US

Thunder Bay

11 17
40
37
61

53

Virginia

165

53
68
54

LAKE SUPERIOR

Isle Royale Nat'l Pk

Copper Harbor

41
45

Houghton

Duluth
Superior
2
210
35

13

Bayfield
Ashland

APOSTLE ISLANDS NATIONAL LAKESHORE

Ontonagon
26

41

Marquette

Ishpeming

MINN
35

35
65

53

13

Hurley Ironwood
MICH 2

50
45

Iron River

46

28

56

Spooner
70

Hayward

Park Falls
70

Eagle River

70

Iron Mountain
Escanaba

32
37

2

St Croix Falls
New Richmond
Hudson
River Falls
94

35
63
38
21
50

Rice Lake
Ladysmith
27

Woodruff

Rhinelander

Crandon

68

141

8

Sister Bay

41
41

53

13

Medford

107 8

Tomahawk
45
51

Merrill
82

59

Antigo
64

Marinette
Menominee
Peshtigo
Oconto

41
42

Sturgeon Bay

Bloomer
Chippewa Falls
53
29
42

Wausau

Shawano
29

19

Green Bay
42

Menomonie
Eau Claire

Marshfield

Durand
Red Wing

52
63

10 69
21
30

77

Neillsville
12

Stevens Pt.

Clintonville
66
New London
45
37

Appleton
39

Kewaunee
Two Rivers
Manitowoc

Whitehall
94

50

Black River Falls
64
55

Wisconsin Rapids
13

Waupaca

Wautoma
21

Neenah
Winnebago

Chilton
57
26

14

Winona
Sparta
Tomah
90

16

Oshkosh
Fond du Lac

Sheboygan

MICHIGAN

La Crosse

Mauston
Adams

Wisconsin Dells
90

Waupun
151

45

43

Port Washington

52
63

MINN
IOWA
Decorah

61
14
1

Viroqua
80

Baraboo

Portage
28

Beaver Dam

Menomonee Falls
76

W Bend

Charles City

18
49

Richland Cen.
52

Spring Green
Columbus
27

Watertown
94

Waukesha

Milwaukee

Oelwein

150

Prairie du Chien
18

Boscobel
18

Dodgeville
151

Lancaster

Madison
Monona
Fort Atkinson
Edgerton
Evansville
69

Whitewater 44

Delavan

Racine

Waterloo

Dubuque

Platteville
11

Janesville
Monroe
28

Geneva
Burlington

Kenosha

380

52
61

ILL
IOWA

20
151
67

Freeport

Beloit
90

109 26

14

39
51

Geneva 12

Waukegan
94

Cedar Rapids

30

80
151

61
17
22
66
30

Clinton

Rockford
85

Elgin
290

Chicago

80

92-1

© R. MSN.

55
88
77

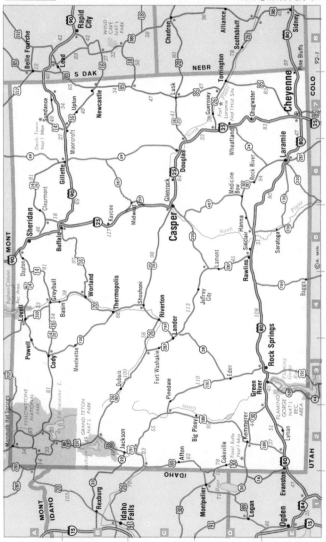

0   100   200   300   400   500 miles

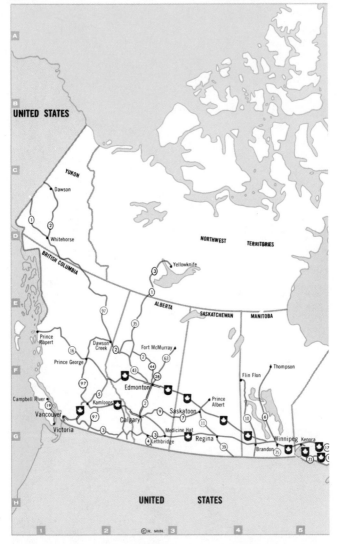

UNITED STATES

YUKON

Dawson

① ②

Whitehorse

BRITISH COLUMBIA

NORTHWEST   TERRITORIES

③

Yellowknife

①

ALBERTA   SASKATCHEWAN   MANITOBA

⑨⑦

③⑤

Prince Rupert

⑯   Dawson Creek   Fort McMurray

Prince George   ②   ②   ㊻   ㊿

⑨⑦   ㊸   ㉘

Campbell River   ⑤   Edmonton

⑲   Kamloops

Vancouver   ②

Victoria   ⑨⑦   Calgary   ⑨   Saskatoon

③   ⑦

Lethbridge   ③   Medicine Hat   ⑪

④   Regina

Prince Albert

Flin Flon   Thompson

⑩   ⑥

Winnipeg   Kenora

Brandon   ⑳⑤   ⑰

㉑   ①

③⑨

UNITED   STATES

© R. McN.   1   2   3   4   5

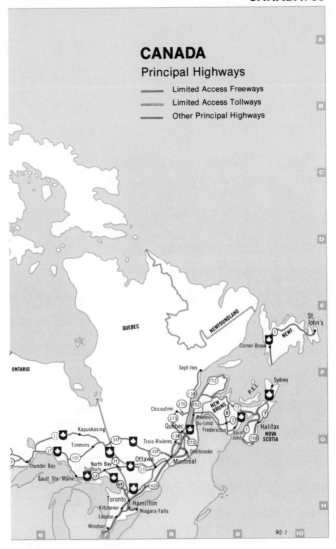

CANADA
Principal Highways

——— Limited Access Freeways
——— Limited Access Tollways
——— Other Principal Highways

QUEBEC

NEWFOUNDLAND

NEWF.

St. John's

Corner Brook

ONTARIO

Sept-Iles

P.E.I.

Sydney

Chicoutimi

NEW BRUNS

Rivière-du-Loup

Québec

Fredericton

Halifax

NOVA SCOTIA

Saint John

Kapuskasing

Trois-Rivières

Timmins

Sherbrooke

Thunder Bay

North Bay

Ottawa

Montréal

Sudbury

Sault Ste. Marie

Toronto

Hamilton

Kitchener

Niagara Falls

London

Windsor

92-1

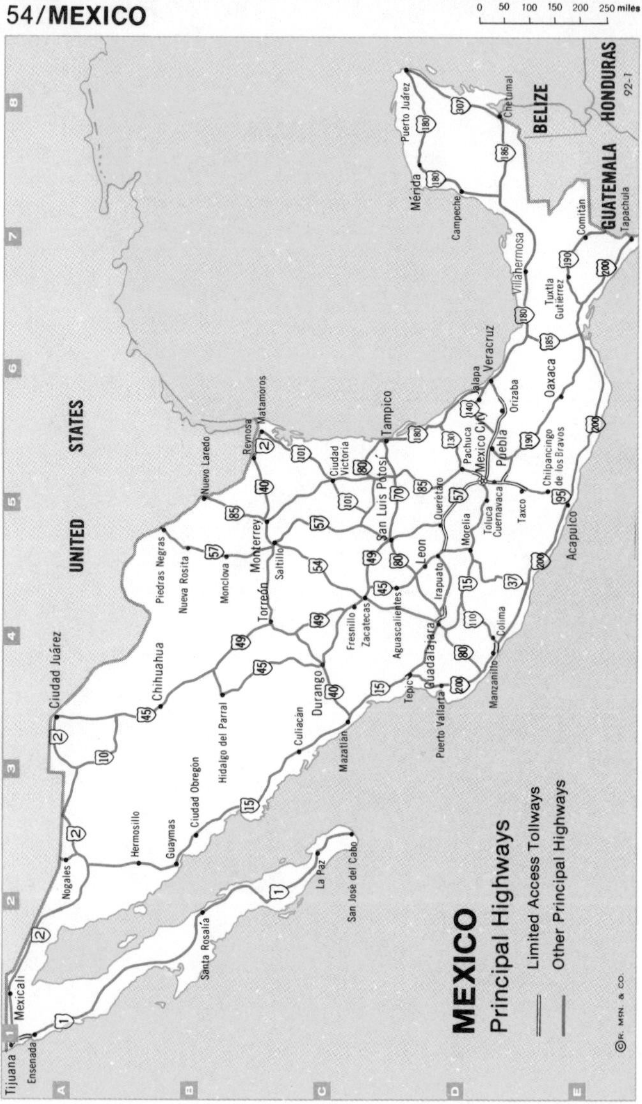

0 50 100 150 200 250 miles
MEXICO
Principal Highways
Limited Access Tollways
Other Principal Highways
©R. McN. & CO.
92-1
UNITED STATES
BELIZE
GUATEMALA
HONDURAS
Tijuana
Ensenada
Mexicali
Nogales
Hermosillo
Guaymas
Ciudad Obregón
Santa Rosalía
La Paz
San José del Cabo
Ciudad Juárez
Chihuahua
Hidalgo del Parral
Culiacán
Mazatlán
Durango
Torreón
Piedras Negras
Nueva Rosita
Monclova
Saltillo
Monterrey
Nuevo Laredo
Reynosa
Matamoros
Ciudad Victoria
Tampico
San Luis Potosí
Fresnillo
Zacatecas
Aguascalientes
Leon
Irapuato
Querétaro
Guadalajara
Tepic
Puerto Vallarta
Colima
Manzanillo
Morelia
Toluca
Cuernavaca
Taxco
Pachuca
Mexico City
Puebla
Jalapa
Veracruz
Orizaba
Oaxaca
Chilpancingo de los Bravos
Acapulco
Villahermosa
Tuxtla Gutiérrez
Comitán
Tapachula
Campeche
Mérida
Puerto Juárez
Chetumal

UNITED STATES MILEAGE CHART

	Albuquerque, N. Mex.	Atlanta, Ga.	Birmingham, Ala.	Boston, Mass.	Chicago, Ill.	Cleveland, Ohio	Dallas, Tex.	Denver, Colo.	Detroit, Mich.	Houston, Tex.	Indianapolis, Ind.	Kansas City, Mo.	Los Angeles, Calif.	Mexico City, Mex.	Miami, Fla.	Minneapolis, Minn.	Montreal, Que.	Nashville, Tenn.	New Orleans, La.	New York, N.Y.	Omaha, Nebr.	Philadelphia, Pa.	Phoenix, Ariz.	Portland, Ore.	St. Louis, Mo.	Salt Lake City, Utah	San Francisco, Calif.	Seattle, Wash.	Toronto, Ont.	Washington, D.C.
Albuquerque, N. Mex.		1404	1254	2220	1372	1585	644	437	1561	853	1267	777	811	1414	1970	1219	2087	1225	1157	1997	889	1947	458	1312	1042	604	1109	1453	1847	1849
Atlanta, Ga.	1404		153	1108	708	728	732	1404	722	789	493	798	2182	1970	663	1108	1219	242	473	854	986	780	1805	2664	555	1934	2483	2625	925	618
Birmingham, Ala.	1254	153		1226	657	732	657	1226	756	701	478	725	2052	1768	754	1068	1270	188	346	978	882	868	1677	2586	512	1791	2365	2540	950	735
Boston, Mass.	2220	1108	1226		994	657	1753	1998	799	1830	929	1435	3017	2783	1520	1390	318	1092	1507	222	1469	315	2670	3144	1207	2376	3144	3016	539	448
Chicago, Ill.	1372	708	657	994		348	921	1091	279	1091	181	542	2048	2045	1397	410	828	466	919	809	479	785	1742	2117	289	1417	2173	2052	492	709
Cleveland, Ohio	1585	728	732	657	348		1189	1362	169	1306	318	819	2382	2251	1252	758	561	533	1055	471	825	428	2032	2432	579	1762	2483	2391	287	360
Dallas, Tex.	644	732	657	1753	921	1189		784	1156	276	892	505	1399	1138	1343	494	1705	664	517	1559	662	1443	1002	2043	655	1257	1752	2131	1369	1307
Denver, Colo.	437	1404	1226	1998	1091	1362	784		1283	1034	1063	600	1301	1746	2107	920	1815	1184	1277	1794	541	1739	813	1261	863	534	1255	1341	1479	1616
Detroit, Mich.	1561	722	756	799	279	169	1156	1283		1276	284	769	2288	2243	1385	685	562	543	1070	649	734	609	2008	2381	534	1671	2399	2327	226	516
Houston, Tex.	853	789	701	1830	1091	1306	276	1034	1276		995	743	1541	979	1190	1183	1827	780	353	1610	864	1511	1164	2237	839	1442	1911	2369	1491	1365
Indianapolis, Ind.	1267	493	478	929	181	318	892	1063	284	995		487	1965	1186	593	840	283	802	731	713	606	725	1435	1725	237	1446	1566	2289	504	575
Kansas City, Mo.	777	798	725	1435	542	819	505	600	769	743	487		1577	1627	1481	443	1305	578	839	1233	189	1170	1235	1820	256	1105	1861	1858	969	1042
Los Angeles, Calif.	811	2182	2052	3017	2048	2382	1399	1301	2288	1541	1965	1577		1876	2757	2073	2896	1857	2873	2805	1747	2874	376	962	1836	691	381	1134	2537	2646
Mexico City, Mex.	1414	1970	1768	2783	2045	2251	1138	1746	2243	979	1186	1627	1876		1965	1627	2169	1684	1217	2587	1334	2587	1549	2785	1757	2016	2291	2852	2469	2354
Miami, Fla.	1970	663	754	1520	1397	1252	1343	2107	1385	1190	593	1481	2757	1965		1786	1654	910	860	1334	1769	1226	2348	3257	1226	2566	3093	3303	1509	1057
Minneapolis, Minn.	1219	1108	1068	1390	410	758	494	920	685	1183	593	443	2073	1627	1786		1163	860	1334	1217	378	1217	1674	1230	561	1195	1677	1630	897	1090
Montreal, Que.	2087	1219	1270	318	828	561	1705	1815	562	1827	283	1305	2896	2169	1654	1163		1074	1163	378	1378	449	2519	2755	1195	2209	2961	2841	336	579
Nashville, Tenn.	1225	242	188	1092	466	533	664	1184	543	780	283	578	1857	1684	910	860	1074		532	900	764	787	1674	2369	321	1703	2325	2442	754	659
New Orleans, La.	1157	473	346	1507	919	1055	517	1277	1070	353	731	839	2873	1217	860	1334	1163	532		1335	860	1229	1496	2536	698	1775	2278	2590	1071	1099
New York, N.Y.	1997	854	978	222	809	471	1559	1794	649	1610	713	1233	2805	2587	1334	1217	378	900	1335		1335	1026	2536	2914	978	2189	2930	2841	469	237
Omaha, Nebr.	889	986	882	1469	479	825	662	541	734	864	606	189	1747	1334	1769	378	1378	764	860	1335		1335	1026	1229	444	936	1691	1692	942	1135
Philadelphia, Pa.	1947	780	868	315	785	428	1443	1739	609	1511	725	1170	2874	2587	1226	1217	449	787	1229	1026	1335		2445	2914	904	2154	2902	2816	453	143
Phoenix, Ariz.	458	1805	1677	2670	1742	2032	1002	813	2008	1164	1435	1235	376	1549	2348	1674	2519	1674	1496	2536	1026	2445		1481	1481	645	762	1485	2183	2300
Portland, Ore.	1312	2664	2586	3144	2117	2432	2043	1261	2381	2237	1725	1820	962	2785	3257	1230	2755	2369	2536	2914	1229	2914	1481		2057	763	637	174	2566	2784
St. Louis, Mo.	1042	555	512	1207	289	579	655	863	534	839	237	256	1836	1757	1226	561	1195	321	698	978	444	904	1481	2057		1481	2118	2135	739	862
Salt Lake City, Utah	604	1934	1791	2376	1417	1762	1257	534	1671	1442	1446	1105	691	2016	2566	1195	2209	1703	1775	2189	936	2154	645	763	1362		752	848	1873	2048
San Francisco, Calif.	1109	2483	2365	3144	2173	2483	1752	1255	2399	1645	1566	1861	381	2291	3093	1677	2961	2325	2278	2930	1691	2902	762	637	2118	752		810	2625	2843
Seattle, Wash.	1453	2625	2540	3016	2052	2391	2131	1341	2327	1911	2289	1858	1134	2852	3303	1630	2841	2442	2590	2841	1692	2816	1485	174	2135	848	810		2496	2721
Toronto, Ont.	1847	925	950	539	492	287	1369	1479	226	1491	504	969	2537	2469	1509	897	336	754	1071	469	942	453	2183	2566	739	1873	2625	2496		456
Washington, D.C.	1849	618	735	448	709	360	1307	1616	516	1365	575	1042	2646	2354	1057	1090	579	659	1099	237	1135	143	2300	2784	862	2048	2843	2721	456	

Mileages Copyright © by Rand McNally-TDM, Inc.

ALABAMA

(Map on page 4)
Pop.: 4,062,608
(1990 Census)
Area: 50,766 Sq. Mi.
Capital: Montgomery

Albertville ... B-4
Alexander City D-4
Andalusia ... G-3
Anniston C-4
Athens A-3
Atmore G-2
Bay Minette .. G-2
Bessemer C-3
Birmingham . C-3
Cullman B-3
Decatur A-3
Demopolis .. E-2
Dothan G-5
Enterprise .. G-4
Eufaula F-5
Florala G-4
Florence A-2
Gadsden B-4
Greenville ... F-3
Guntersville . B-3
Homewood ... C-3
Huntsville ... A-3
Jacksonville . C-4
Leeds C-3
Mobile H-1
Montgomery . E-3
Muscle Shoals A-2
Opelika D-5
Prichard G-1
Saraland G-1
Selma E-3
Sylacauga .. B-4
Talladega ... C-4
Tarrant City .. C-3
Thomasville . F-2
Troy F-4
Tuscaloosa .. D-2
Tuscumbia. .. A-2
Tuskegee ... E-4

ALASKA

(Map on page 5)
Pop.: 551,947
(1990 Census)
Area: 570,833 Sq. Mi.
Capital: Juneau

Anchorage .. C-3
Barrow A-3
Bethel C-2
Cordova C-3
Fairbanks ... B-3
Juneau C-5
Kenai C-3
Ketchikan ... D-5
Nome B-2
Petersburg .. D-5
Port Heiden.. D-2

Sitka D-5
Spenard C-3
Valdez C-3

ARIZONA

(Map on page 6-7)
Pop.: 3,677,985
(1990 Census)
Area: 113,510 Sq. Mi.
Capital: Phoenix

Ajo G-2
Avondale F-3
Bisbee H-5
Casa Grande . F-3
Coolidge F-3
Douglas H-5
Flagstaff D-3
Gila Bend ... F-2
Glendale E-3
Globe F-4
Grand Canyon C-3
Lake Havasu
    City D-1
Mesa F-3
Morenci F-5
Nogales H-4
Page B-4
Phoenix E-3
Prescott D-3
Safford F-5
Scottsdale .. F-3
Sun City E-3
Tempe F-3
Tucson G-4
Winslow D-4
Yuma F-1

ARKANSAS

(Map on page 8-9)
Pop.: 2,362,239
(1990 Census)
Area: 52,082 Sq. Mi.
Capital: Little Rock

Arkadelphia . D-3
Batesville ... B-4
Blytheville .. A-6
Booneville .. B-2
Camden D-3
Clarksville .. B-2
Conway C-3
Crossett E-4
Danville C-2
El Dorado ... E-3
Eudora E-5
Fayetteville . A-1
Forrest City .. C-5
Ft. Smith B-1
Harrison A-3
Helena C-5
Hope D-2
Hot Sprs.
    Nat'l. Pk. .. C-3
Jacksonville . C-4

Jonesboro ... B-5
Lake Village . E-5
Little Rock ... C-4
Magnolia E-2
Marianna C-5
Marked Tree . B-6
Mena C-1
Morrilton B-3
Newport B-5
N. Little Rock . C-4
Paragould ... A-6
Pine Bluff ... D-4
Russellville .. B-3
Salem A-4
Springdale .. A-2
Stuttgart C-4
Texarkana ... D-2
Van Buren .. B-1
Warren D-4
W. Memphis . B-6

CALIFORNIA

(Map on page 10-11)
Pop.: 29,839,250
(1990 Census)
Area: 156,297 Sq. Mi.
Capital: Sacramento

Anaheim J-5
Atwater E-3
Auburn D-3
Bakersfield .. G-5
Barstow H-6
Berkeley E-2
Blythe J-8
Chula Vista .. K-6
Clovis F-4
Davis D-3
El Cajon K-6
El Centro K-7
Eureka B-1
Fairfield D-2
Fremont E-2
Fresno F-4
Glendale H-5
Hollister F-3
Lancaster ... H-5
Long Beach ..J-5
Los Angeles ..J-5
Los Banos .. F-3
Madera F-4
Merced E-3
Modesto E-3
Monterey ... F-2
Napa D-2
Newport
    Beach J-5
Novato E-2
Oakland E-2
Oceanside ...J-6
Oroville C-3
Oxnard H-4
Palm Springs .J-6
Palo Alto ... E-2
Paradise C-3
Pasadena ... H-5

Placerville ... D-3
Pomona J-5
Redding B-2
Richmond ... E-2
Riverside J-6
Sacramento . D-3
Salinas F-3
San
    Bernardino H-6
San Diego ... K-6
San Francisco E-2
San Jose ... E-2
San Luis
    Obispo ... G-3
San Mateo ... E-2
Santa Ana ...J-5
Santa Barbara H-4
Santa Cruz .. F-2
Santa Monica .J-5
Santa Rosa .. D-2
South Lake
    Tahoe D-4
Stockton E-3
Susanville ... B-3
Turlock E-3
Ukiah D-1
Vallejo E-2
Ventura H-4
Visalia F-4
Watsonville .. F-2
Woodland ... D-3
Yreka A-2
Yuba City ... D-3

COLORADO

(Map on page 14)
Pop.: 3,307,912
(1990 Census)
Area: 103,598 Sq. Mi.
Capital: Denver

Alamosa E-4
Aspen C-3
Aurora B-5
Boulder B-5
Brighton B-5
Canon City .. D-5
Cimarron ... E-2
Colorado
    Springs ... C-5
Cortez E-2
Craig A-3
Delta C-2
Denver B-5
Durango E-2
Englewood .. B-5
Ft. Collins ... A-5
Ft. Morgan .. B-6
Glenwood
    Springs ... B-3
Grand
    Junction .. C-2
Greeley A-5
Gunnison ... C-3
La Junta D-6
Lakewood ... B-5

Lamar D-7
Leadville ... C-4
Limon C-6
Longmont .. B-5
Loveland ... A-5
Manitou Sprs. C-5
Meeker B-2
Montrose ... D-2
Pueblo D-5
Rocky Ford . D-6
Salida C-4
Silverton ... D-3
Steamboat
  Springs ... A-3
Sterling A-7
Trinidad E-6
Vail B-4
Walsenburg . E-5

CONNECTICUT

(Map on page 12-13)
Pop.: 3,295,669
(1990 Census)
Area: 4,872 Sq. Mi.
Capital: Hartford

Bridgeport .. G-2
Bristol F-2
Enfield D-4
Fairfield G-2
Greenwich .. H-1
Groton G-5
Hamden G-3
Hartford E-3
Manchester . E-4
Meriden F-3
Middletown . F-3
Milford G-2
New Britain . F-3
New Haven . G-3
New London . G-5
Norwalk G-1
Norwich F-5
Putnam E-5
Seymour G-3
Stamford ... H-1
Stratford ... G-2
Torrington .. E-2
Trumbull ... G-2
Wallingford . F-3
Waterbury .. F-2
W. Hartford . E-3
Willimantic .. E-4
Windsor
  Locks E-3
Winsted E-2

DELAWARE

(Map on page 24-25)
Pop.: 668,696
(1990 Census)
Area: 1,933 Sq. Mi.
Capital: Dover

Dover C-10
Laurel D-10

Lewes D-10
Milford D-10
Newark B-9
Seaford ... D-10
Smyrna ... C-10
Wilmington . B-10

DISTRICT OF COLUMBIA

(Map on page 24-25)
Pop.: 609,909
(1990 Census)
Area: 69 Sq. Mi.

Washington . C-5

FLORIDA

(Map on page 15)
Pop.: 13,003,362
(1990 Census)
Area: 54,157 Sq. Mi.
Capital: Tallahassee

Arcadia E-3
Bartow D-3
Belle Glade . F-5
Boca Raton .. F-5
Boynton
  Beach F-5
Bradenton ... E-3
Chattahoochee
  .... A-1,G-3
Clearwater .. D-3
Cocoa D-4
Coral Gables . G-5
Crestview ... G-2
Daytona
  Beach C-4
De Land C-4
Delray Beach F-5
Dunedin D-3
Ft. Lauderdale . F-5
Ft. Myers F-3
Ft. Pierce ... E-5
Ft. Walton
  Beach G-2
Gainesville .. B-3
Greenville .. A-2
Hialeah F-5
Hollywood .. F-5
Jacksonville . B-4
Jacksonville
  Beach B-4
Key West ... H-3
Lake City ... B-3
Lakeland ... D-3
Lake Wales .. D-4
Lake Worth .. F-5
Leesburg ... C-3
Marathon ... H-4
Melbourne .. D-5
Miami G-5
Miami Beach G-5
Naples F-4
Ocala C-3

Orlando C-4
Ormond
  Beach C-4
Palatka B-4
Panama City . H-3
Pensacola .. G-1
Perry B-2
Plant City ... D-3
Pompano
  Beach F-5
Riviera
  Beach E-5
St. Augustine B-4
St. PetersburgD-3
Sanford C-4
Sarasota E-3
Sebring E-3
Tallahassee . A-1
Tampa D-3
Titusville ... C-4
Venice E-3
Vero Beach .. D-5
W. Palm
  Beach E-5
W. Pensacola G-1
Winter Haven D-4
Winter Park .. C-4

GEORGIA

(Map on page 16)
Pop.: 6,508,419
(1990 Census)
Area: 58,060 Sq. Mi.
Capital: Atlanta

Albany F-2
Americus E-2
Athens C-3
Atlanta C-2
Augusta D-4
Bainbridge .. G-2
Baxley F-4
Blakely F-1
Brunswick .. F-5
Cairo G-2
Carrollton ... D-1
Clayton B-3
Columbus .. E-1
Cordele E-2
Covington .. D-2
Dahlonega .. B-2
Dalton B-1
Decatur C-2
Dublin E-3
Fitzgerald .. F-3
Gainesville .. C-2
Griffin D-2
Jesup F-4
La Grange .. D-1
Macon D-3
McRae E-3
Marietta C-2
Milledgeville . D-3
Monroe C-2
Moultrie F-2
Newnan D-1
Perry E-2

Rome C-1
Savannah ... E-5
Statesboro .. E-4
Thomasville . G-2
Tifton F-3
Valdosta ... G-3
Warner
  Robins ... E-3
Waycross ... F-4
Waynesboro . D-4

HAWAII

(Map on page 5)
Pop.: 1,115,274
(1990 Census)
Area: 6,427 Sq. Mi.
Capital: Honolulu

Hilo G-5
Honolulu F-3
Kahana G-2
Kahului F-4
Kailua F-3
Kaneohe ... F-3
Kapaa E-2
Kawela F-2
Lahaina F-4
Nanakuli ... G-1
Pearl City ... F-3
Puuanahulu . G-4
Puunene F-4
Wahiawa ... G-2
Wailuku F-4

IDAHO

(Map on page 17)
Pop.: 1,011,986
(1990 Census)
Area: 82,413 Sq. Mi.
Capital: Boise

American
  Falls G-4
Blackfoot ... G-4
Boise F-1
Bonners Ferry A-1
Burley H-3
Caldwell ... F-1
Coeur d'Alene B-1
Grangeville .. D-1
Idaho Falls .. F-4
Jerome G-3
Kellogg B-2
Lewiston ... C-1
Montpelier .. H-5
Moscow C-1
Nampa F-1
Payette F-1
Pocatello ... G-4
Preston H-5
Rexburg F-5
St. Anthony . F-5
Shelley G-4
Sun Valley .. F-3
Twin Falls ... G-3
Weise F-1

58

ILLINOIS
(Map on page 18)
Pop.: 11,466,682
(1990 Census)
Area: 55,646 Sq. Mi.
Capital: Springfield

Alton	F-2
Arlington Hts.	A-4
Aurora	B-4
Belleville	F-2
Belvidere	A-4
Bloomington	D-3
Cairo	H-3
Carbondale	G-3
Carmi	G-4
Centralia	F-3
Champaign	D-4
Charleston	E-4
Chicago	A-5
Chicago Heights	B-5
Collinsville	F-2
Danville	D-5
Decatur	D-4
De Kalb	A-4
Dixon	B-3
East St. Louis	F-2
Effingham	E-4
Elgin	A-4
Evanston	A-5
Freeport	A-3
Galena	A-2
Galesburg	C-2
Harrisburg	G-4
Highland Park	A-5
Jacksonville	E-2
Joliet	B-4
Kankakee	C-5
Kewanee	B-3
Lincoln	D-3
Macomb	D-2
Marion	G-4
Marshall	E-5
Mattoon	E-4
Moline	B-2
Monmouth	C-2
Mt. Carmel	F-5
Mt. Vernon	G-4
Nauvoo	C-1
Newton	F-4
Normal	C-3
Ottawa	B-4
Pekin	C-3
Peoria	C-3
Peru	B-3
Pittsfield	E-2
Pontiac	C-4
Quincy	D-1
Rantoul	D-4
Rock Falls	B-3
Rockford	A-3
Rock Island	B-2
Springfield	D-3
Sterling	B-3
Streator	C-4
Urbana	D-4
Vandalia	F-3

Watseka	C-5
Waukegan	A-5
W. Frankfort	G-4
Woodstock	A-4

INDIANA
(Map on page 19)
Pop.: 5,564,228
(1990 Census)
Area: 35,936 Sq. Mi.
Capital: Indianapolis

Anderson	D-4
Angola	A-5
Bedford	F-3
Bloomington	F-3
Brazil	E-2
Clinton	E-2
Columbus	F-4
Connersville	E-5
Crawfordsville	D-2
Crown Point	A-2
Decatur	B-5
Elkhart	A-4
Elwood	D-4
Evansville	H-1
Fort Wayne	B-5
Frankfort	D-3
Franklin	E-4
French Lick	G-3
Gary	A-2
Goshen	A-4
Greencastle	E-2
Greenfield	D-4
Griffith	A-2
Hammond	A-2
Hartford City	C-5
Huntington	B-4
Indianapolis	E-3
Kokomo	C-3
Lafayette	C-2
La Porte	A-3
Lebanon	D-3
Logansport	C-3
Madison	F-5
Marion	C-4
Martinsville	E-3
Michigan City	A-2
Mishawaka	A-3
Muncie	D-4
New Albany	G-4
New Castle	D-5
Noblesville	D-4
Peru	C-4
Plymouth	A-3
Portage	A-2
Portland	C-5
Princeton	G-1
Richmond	D-5
Rockport	H-2
Rockville	E-2
Scottsburg	G-4
Seymour	F-4
Shelbyville	E-4
South Bend	A-3
Terre Haute	E-2
Valparaiso	A-2

Versailles	F-5
Wabash	C-4
Warsaw	B-4
Washington	G-2
W. Lafayette	C-2

IOWA
(Map on page 20)
Pop.: 2,787,424
(1990 Census)
Area: 55,965 Sq. Mi.
Capital: Des Moines

Ames	C-4
Atlantic	D-3
Burlington	E-7
Cedar Falls	B-6
Cedar Rapids	C-6
Centerville	C-5
Charles City	A-5
Cherokee	B-2
Clinton	C-8
Council Bluffs	D-2
Creston	D-3
Davenport	D-8
Decorah	A-6
Des Moines	D-4
Dubuque	B-8
Estherville	A-3
Fairfield	D-6
Ft. Dodge	B-4
Ft. Madison	E-7
Grinnell	C-5
Iowa City	C-7
Knoxville	D-5
Le Mars	B-1
Marshalltown	C-5
Mason City	A-5
Muscatine	D-7
Newton	C-5
Oelwein	B-6
Oskaloosa	D-5
Ottumwa	D-6
Red Oak	D-2
Rock Rapids	A-1
Shenandoah	E-2
Sioux City	B-1
Spencer	A-2
Storm Lake	B-2
Washington	D-6
Waterloo	B-6
Webster City	B-4

KANSAS
(Map on page 21)
Pop.: 2,485,600
(1990 Census)
Area: 81,783 Sq. Mi.
Capital: Topeka

Abilene	C-6
Atchison	B-8
Belleville	A-5
Chanute	D-7

Colby	B-2
Concordia	B-5
Dodge City	D-3
El Dorado	D-6
Emporia	C-7
Ft. Scott	D-8
Garden City	D-2
Goodland	B-1
Great Bend	C-4
Hays	C-3
Hutchinson	D-5
Independence	E-7
Junction City	B-6
Kansas City	B-8
Lawrence	B-8
Leavenworth	B-8
Liberal	E-2
McPherson	C-5
Manhattan	B-6
Marysville	A-6
Oakley	B-2
Olathe	C-8
Ottawa	C-8
Parsons	D-8
Phillipsburg	B-3
Pittsburg	D-8
Pratt	D-4
St. Francis	A-1
Salina	C-5
Syracuse	D-1
Topeka	B-7
Tribune	C-1
Wellington	E-5
Wichita	D-5
Winfield	E-6

KENTUCKY
(Map on page 22-23)
Pop.: 3,698,969
(1990 Census)
Area: 39,674 Sq. Mi.
Capital: Frankfort

Ashland	B-9
Barbourville	E-8
Bardstown	C-6
Beaver Dam	D-4
Berea	D-7
Bowling Green	E-5
Columbia	D-6
Corbin	E-8
Covington	B-7
Cumberland	E-9
Danville	D-7
Elizabethtown	D-6
Frankfort	C-7
Fulton	E-2
Glasgow	E-6
Harrodsburg	C-7
Hazard	D-9
Henderson	C-4
Hodgenville	D-6
Hopkinsville	E-4
Lawrenceburg	C-7

Lexington ... C-7
Louisville C-6
Madisonville . D-4
Mayfield E-3
Maysville B-8
Middlesboro . E-8
Morehead C-8
Morgantown . D-5
Murray E-3
Newport B-7
Owensboro .. C-4
Paducah D-3
Paris C-7
Pikeville D-9
Pineville E-8
Prestonsburg D-9
Richmond ... C-7
Salyersville .. C-9
Somerset D-7

LOUISIANA

(Map on page 8-9)
Pop.: 4,238,216
(1990 Census)
Area: 44,520 Sq. Mi.
Capital: Baton Rouge

Abbeville J-4
Alexandria .. G-3
Baton Rouge H-5
Bogalusa H-6
Bossier City . F-2
Chalmette J-6
Crowley J-4
Eunice H-4
Hammond H-6
Jennings J-3
Lafayette J-4
Lake Charles .J-2
Metairie J-6
Monroe F-4
Morgan City .J-5
Natchitoches G-3
New Iberia ...J-4
New Orleans ..J-6
Opelousas .. H-4
Port Sulphur . K-7
Ruston F-3
Shreveport .. F-2
Sulphur J-2
Tallulah F-5
Winnfield G-3

MAINE

(Map on page 26)
Pop.: 1,233,223
(1990 Census)
Area: 30,995 Sq. Mi.
Capital: Augusta

Auburn F-2
Augusta F-2
Bangor E-3
Biddeford ... G-1
Brewer E-3
Brunswick ... G-2

Caribou B-4
Eastport E-5
Ellsworth F-4
Fort Kent A-3
Gardiner F-2
Houlton C-4
Jackman D-2
Lewiston F-2
Madawaska . A-4
Mattawamkeag
.... D-4
Pittsfield E-3
Portland G-2
Presque Isle . B-4
Rangeley E-1
Rockland F-3
Saco H-1
Skowhegan . E-2
Waterville ... F-2
Westbrook ... G-1

MARYLAND

(Map on page 24-25)
Pop.: 4,798,622
(1990 Census)
Area: 9,838 Sq. Mi.
Capital: Annapolis

Aberdeen ... C-9
Annapolis ... C-9
Baltimore ... C-9
Bel Air C-9
Cambridge .. D-9
Cumberland . C-6
Easton D-9
Frederick ... C-8
Frostburg ... C-6
Hagerstown . C-7
La Plata D-8
Lexington
Park D-9
Oakland C-6
Ocean City . D-10
Pocomoke
City E-10
Reisterstown C-8
Rockville ... C-8
Salisbury ... D-10
Westminster . C-8

MASSACHUSETTS

(Map on page 12-13)
Pop.: 6,029,051
(1990 Census)
Area: 7,826 Sq. Mi.
Capital: Boston

Adams B-2
Athol B-4
Attleboro E-7
Boston C-7
Brockton D-8
Cambridge .. C-7
Chicopee D-3
Edgartown ... F-9

Fall River E-7
Fitchburg ... B-6
Framingham . C-7
Gardner B-5
Gloucester .. B-8
Grafton D-6
Greenfield .. B-3
Haverhill B-7
Holyoke D-3
Hyannis E-9
Lawrence ... B-7
Leominster .. C-6
Lexington ... C-7
Lowell B-7
Lynn C-8
Marlboro C-6
Milford D-6
New Bedford F 8
N. Adams ... B-2
Northampton C-3
Pittsfield ... C-2
Provincetown
.... D-10
Quincy D-8
Southbridge . D-5
Springfield .. D-4
Webster D-5
Westfield D-3
Weymouth .. D-8
Woburn C-7
Worcester ... C-6

MICHIGAN

(Map on page 27)
Pop.: 9,328,784
(1990 Census)
Area: 56,959 Sq. Mi.
Capital: Lansing

Albion G-3
Alpena D-4
Ann Arbor .. G-4
Battle Creek . G-3
Bay City E-4
Benton
Harbor G-2
Birmingham . G-5
Cadillac E-3
Dearborn G-5
Detroit G-5
Escanaba ... C-1
Flint F-4
Grand Haven F-2
Grand Rapids F-2
Hillsdale H-3
Holland G-2
Iron Mountain B-1
Ishpeming .. B-1
Jackson G-4
Kalamazoo .. G-2
Lansing G-3
Livonia G-4
Ludington ... E-2
Mackinaw ... C-3
Marquette .. B-1
Menominee . C-1
Midland E-4

Monroe H-4
Mount
Clemens... G-5
Muskegon .. F-2
Niles H-2
Owosso F-4
Pontiac G-5
Portage G-2
Port Huron .. F-5
Saginaw F-4
Sault Ste.
Marie B-4
Three Rivers . H-2
Traverse City D-2
Trenton G-5
Ypsilanti H-4

MINNESOTA

(Map on page 28)
Pop.: 4,387,029
(1990 Census)
Area: 79,548 Sq. Mi.
Capital: St. Paul

Albert Lea ... H-4
Alexandria .. E-2
Austin H-4
Bemidji C-2
Bloomington F-4
Brainerd E-3
Cambridge .. F-4
Chisholm ... C-4
Cloquet D-4
Crookston ... C-1
Duluth D-5
E. Grand
Forks C-1
Ely C-5
Fairmont H-3
Faribault G-4
Fergus Falls . E-1
Hibbing C-4
Hutchinson . F-3
International
Falls B-3
Mankato G-3
Marshall G-2
Minneapolis . F-4
Moorhead .. D-1
New Ulm G-3
Northfield ... G-4
Owatonna ... H-4
Pine City E-4
Rochester ... G-4
Roseau B-2
St. Cloud ... F-3
St. Paul F-4
St. Peter G-3
Sandstone .. E-4
Stillwater ... F-4
Thief River
Falls C-1
Virginia C-4
White Bear
Lake F-4
Willmar F-2
Winona G-5
Worthington . H-2

MISSISSIPPI

(Map on page 8-9)
Pop.: 2,586,443
(1990 Census)
Area: 47,234 Sq. Mi.
Capital: Jackson

Aberdeen	D-8
Biloxi	H-8
Booneville	C-8
Brookhaven	G-6
Canton	F-6
Clarksdale	D-6
Cleveland	D-5
Columbia	G-6
Columbus	D-8
Corinth	C-8
Greenville	E-5
Greenwood	D-6
Grenada	D-6
Gulfport	H-7
Hattiesburg	G-7
Holly Sprs.	C-7
Indianola	D-5
Jackson	F-6
Kosciusko	E-7
Laurel	G-7
Louisville	E-7
McComb	G-6
Mendenhall	F-6
Meridian	F-8
Moss Pt.	H-8
Natchez	G-5
New Albany	C-7
Oxford	C-7
Pascagoula	H-8
Philadelphia	E-7
Quitman	F-8
Senatobia	C-6
Starkville	D-7
Tupelo	C-8
Vicksburg	F-5
Winona	D-6
Woodville	H-5
Yazoo City	E-6

MISSOURI

(Map on page 29)
Pop.: 5,137,804
(1990 Census)
Area: 68,945 Sq. Mi.
Capital: Jefferson City

Bethany	A-3
Bismarck	D-6
Boonville	B-4
Cape Girardeau	D-7
Carthage	D-3
Chillicothe	B-4
Columbia	B-5
Eldon	C-4
Excelsior Springs	B-3
Festus	C-6
Fulton	C-5
Hannibal	B-5

Independence	B-3
Jefferson City	C-5
Joplin	D-3
Kansas City	B-3
Kennett	E-6
Kirksville	A-4
Lees Summit	B-3
Marshall	B-4
Mexico	B-5
Milan	A-4
Moberly	B-4
Mound City	A-2
Nevada	D-3
New Madrid	E-7
Palmyra	B-5
Piedmont	D-6
Poplar Bluff	E-6
Rolla	C-5
St. Charles	C-6
St. Joseph	B-3
St. Louis	C-6
Salem	D-5
Sedalia	C-4
Sikeston	D-7
Springfield	D-4
Warrensburg	C-3
W. Plains	E-5

MONTANA

(Map on page 30)
Pop.: 803,655
(1990 Census)
Area: 145,388 Sq. Mi.
Capital: Helena

Anaconda	D-3
Billings	D-5
Bozeman	D-4
Browning	A-3
Butte	D-3
Columbia Falls	A-2
Deer Lodge	C-3
Dillon	D-3
Ekalaka	D-8
Eureka	A-1
Glasgow	B-7
Glendive	C-8
Great Falls	B-4
Hardin	D-6
Harlem	A-5
Havre	A-5
Helena	C-3
Kalispell	B-2
Lewistown	C-5
Libby	A-1
Livingston	D-4
Miles City	C-7
Missoula	C-2
Phillipsburg	C-2
Roundup	C-5
Shelby	A-3
Superior	C-1
Thompson Falls	B-1
Whitefish	A-2
Wolf Pt.	B-7

NEBRASKA

(Map on page 31)
Pop.: 1,584,617
(1990 Census)
Area: 76,639 Sq. Mi.
Capital: Lincoln

Ainsworth	B-4
Alliance	B-2
Alma	E-5
Auburn	D-8
Bayard	C-1
Beatrice	D-7
Blair	C-8
Bridgeport	C-1
Broken Bow	C-4
Crawford	A-1
Fairbury	D-7
Falls City	D-8
Fremont	C-7
Gering	B-1
Grand Island	D-6
Hastings	D-6
Holdrege	D-5
Kimball	C-1
Lincoln	D-7
Loup City	C-5
McCook	D-4
Nebraska City	D-8
Neligh	B-6
Norfolk	B-6
North Platte	C-4
Ogallala	C-3
Omaha	C-8
O'Neill	B-5
Oshkosh	C-2
Plattsmouth	C-8
Red Cloud	D-6
Rushville	A-2
Scottsbluff	B-1
Seward	D-7
Sidney	C-1
Syracuse	D-8
Valentine	A-4
Wayne	B-7
York	D-6

NEVADA

(Map on page 10-11)
Pop.: 1,206,152
(1990 Census)
Area: 109,895 Sq. Mi.
Capital: Carson City

Austin	C-6
Babbitt	D-5
Battle Mtn.	B-6
Boulder City	G-8
Carlin	B-7
Carson City	D-4
Elko	B-7
Ely	C-8
Empire	B-4
Eureka	C-7
Fallon	C-5
Hawthorne	D-5

Henderson	G-8
Indian Sprs.	F-7
Las Vegas	G-8
Lovelock	C-5
N. Las Vegas	F-8
Overton	F-8
Reno	C-4
Sparks	C-4
Tonopah	E-6
Warm Sprs.	D-7
Wells	B-7
Winnemucca	B-5
Yerington	D-4

NEW HAMPSHIRE

(Map on page 32)
Pop.: 1,113,915
(1990 Census)
Area: 8,992 Sq. Mi.
Capital: Concord

Ashland	E-4
Berlin	C-4
Bristol	E-4
Center Ossipee	E-5
Claremont	F-3
Colebrook	B-4
Concord	F-4
Conway	D-5
Derry	G-4
Dover	F-5
Franklin	E-4
Hampton	G-5
Keene	G-3
Laconia	E-4
Lebanon	E-3
Littleton	C-3
Manchester	G-4
Nashua	G-4
N. Woodstock	D-4
Peterborough	G-3
Portsmouth	F-5
Rochester	F-5
Salem	G-4
Winchester	G-3
Woodsville	D-4

NEW JERSEY

(Map on page 33)
Pop.: 7,748,634
(1990 Census)
Area: 7,468 Sq. Mi.
Capital: Trenton

Asbury Park	D-5
Atlantic City	G-4
Bayonne	C-4
Bloomfield	B-4
Bridgeton	G-2
Burlington	E-3
Camden	E-2
Clifton	B-4

OHIO *Cont'd*

Parma	C-6
Portsmouth	J-4
Ravenna	D-7
Salem	D-8
Sandusky	C-4
Shaker Hts.	C-7
Springfield	G-2
Steubenville	E-8
Toledo	B-3
Troy	F-2
Van Wert	D-1
Warren	C-8
Washington C.H.	G-3
Wilmington	H-2
Wooster	D-6
Youngstown	D-8
Zanesville	G-6

OKLAHOMA

(Map on page 39)
Pop.: 3,157,604
(1990 Census)
Area: 68,656 Sq. Mi.
Capital: Oklahoma City

Ada	C-6
Altus	C-4
Alva	A-5
Anadarko	C-5
Ardmore	D-6
Atoka	D-7
Bartlesville	A-7
Blackwell	A-6
Boise City	A-1
Chickasha	C-5
Clinton	B-4
Cushing	B-6
Duncan	C-5
Durant	D-7
Elk City	B-4
Enid	A-5
Guthrie	B-6
Guymon	A-2
Henryetta	B-6
Hugo	D-7
Idabel	D-8
Lawton	C-5
McAlester	C-7
Miami	A-8
Midwest City	B-6
Muskogee	B-7
Norman	C-6
Oklahoma City	B-6
Okmulgee	B-7
Ponca City	A-6
Sapulpa	B-7
Seminole	C-6
Shawnee	C-6
Stillwater	B-6
Tulsa	B-7
Waynoka	A-4
Weatherford	B-4
Woodward	A-4

OREGON

(Map on page 44)
Pop.: 2,853,733
(1990 Census)
Area: 96,187 Sq. Mi.
Capital: Salem

Albany	B-3
Ashland	E-3
Astoria	A-2
Baker	B-7
Bend	C-4
Brookings	E-1
Burns	D-6
Condon	B-5
Coos Bay	D-2
Corvallis	B-2
Dallas	B-2
Enterprise	A-7
Eugene	C-3
Florence	C-2
Forest Grove	B-3
Gold Beach	E-1
Grants Pass	E-2
Hillsboro	B-3
Jordan Valley	D-7
Klamath Falls	E-4
La Grande	B-6
Lakeview	E-5
La Pine	D-4
Medford	E-3
Milton-Freewater	A-6
Newport	B-2
North Bend	D-2
Nyssa	C-7
Ontario	C-7
Oregon City	B-3
Pendleton	A-6
Portland	B-3
Port Orford	D-1
Redmond	C-4
Roseburg	D-2
Salem	B-3
Silver Lake	D-4
Springfield	C-3
The Dalles	B-4

PENNSYLVANIA

(Map on page 42-43)
Pop.: 11,924,710
(1990 Census)
Area: 44,892 Sq. Mi.
Capital: Harrisburg

Allentown	E-9
Altoona	F-4
Beaver Falls	E-I
Bedford	G-4
Berwick	D-8
Bethlehem	E-9
Bloomsburg	D-7
Canonsburg	F-1
Carbondale	C-9
Carlisle	F-6
Chambersburg	G-5
Chester	G-9
Clairton	F-2
Clarion	D-3
Coatesville	G-8
Connellsville	G-2
Du Bois	D-4
Easton	E-9
E. Stroudsburg	D-10
Erie	B-1
Franklin	C-2
Gettysburg	G-7
Glenshaw	E-2
Greensburg	F-2
Hanover	G-7
Harrisburg	F-7
Hazleton	E-8
Indiana	E-3
Johnstown	F-3
Kingston	D-8
Kittanning	E-2
Lancaster	G-8
Lebanon	F-8
Lewistown	E-6
McKeesport	F-2
Mansfield	C-6
Meadville	C-1
Milford	D-10
Mt. Carmel	E-8
New Castle	D-1
Norristown	F-9
Oil City	C-2
Philadelphia	G-10
Pittsburgh	F-2
Pittston	D-8
Port Allegany	C-4
Pottstown	F-9
Pottsville	E-8
Reading	F-8
Ridgway	C-4
Scranton	C-9
Sharon	D-1
State College	E-5
Sunbury	E-7
Titusville	C-2
Towanda	C-7
Uniontown	G-2
Upper Darby	G-9
Warren	C-3
Washington	F-1
Waynesboro	G-6
Wilkes-Barre	D-8
Wilkinsburg	F-2
Williamsport	D-7
York	G-7

RHODE ISLAND

(Map on page 12-13)
Pop.: 1,005,984
(1990 Census)
Area: 1,054 Sq. Mi.
Capital: Providence

Bristol	F-7
Cranston	E-7
Kingston	F-6
Middletown	F-7
Newport	F-7
Pawtucket	E-7
Providence	E-7
Wakefield	F-6
Warwick	E-7
Westerly	G-6
Woonsocket	D-6

SOUTH CAROLINA

(Map on page 36-37)
Pop.: 3,505,707
(1990 Census)
Area: 30,207 Sq. Mi.
Capital: Columbia

Aiken	F-3
Allendale	G-4
Anderson	D-2
Andrews	F-6
Bamberg	F-4
Batesburg	E-4
Beaufort	G-5
Bennettsville	D-6
Charleston	G-5
Clemson	D-2
Clinton	E-3
Columbia	E-4
Conway	E-7
Darlington	E-6
Dillon	E-6
Easley	D-3
Florence	E-6
Gaffney	D-4
Georgetown	F-6
Greenville	D-3
Greer	D-3
Hampton	G-4
Hartsville	E-5
Kingstree	F-6
Lake City	E-6
Lancaster	D-4
Laurens	D-3
Myrtle Beach	F-7
North Augusta	F-3
N. Charleston	G-5
Orangeburg	F-4
Ridgeland	G-4
Rock Hill	D-4
Spartanburg	D-3
Summerville	F-5
Sumter	E-5
Union	D-4
Walterboro	G-5
Whitmire	D-4

SOUTH DAKOTA

(Map on page 45)
Pop.: 699,999
(1990 Census)
Area: 75,956 Sq. Mi.
Capital: Pierre

Rand McNally Pocket World Atlas

Contents

Map Legend

Urban Area (area of continuous industrial, commercial, and residential development)

The size of type indicates the relative economic and political importance of the locality

Écommoy   Lisieux   **Rouen**

Trouville   **Orléans**   **PARIS**

Capitals of Political Units

BUDAPEST   Independent Nation

Cayenne   Dependency (Colony, protectorate, etc.)

Lasa   State, Province, etc.

Alternate Names

MOSKVA
'MOSCOW   English or second official language names are shown in reduced size lettering

Volgograd
(Stalingrad)   Historical or other alternates in the local language are shown in parentheses

Political Boundaries

International (First-order political unit)

—··—··—··   Demarcated and Undemarcated

— — —   Indefinite or Undefined

··········   Demarcation Line (used in Korea)

Internal

▬▬▬   State, Province, etc. (Second-order political unit)

MURCIA   Historical Region (No boundaries indicated)

Transportation

————   Primary Road

————   Secondary Road

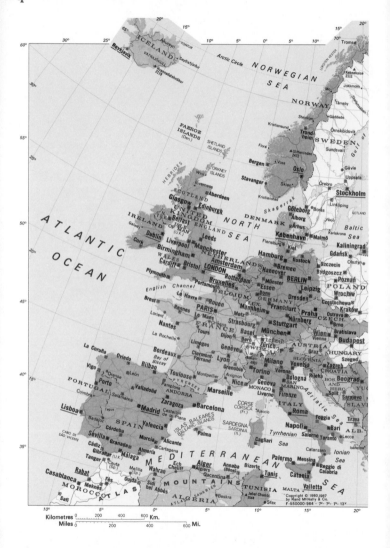

Kilometres 0 200 400 600 Km.
Miles 0 200 400 600 Mi.

Copyright © 1980,1987
by Rand McNally & Co.
F-550000-964 - 7° - 7° - 13°

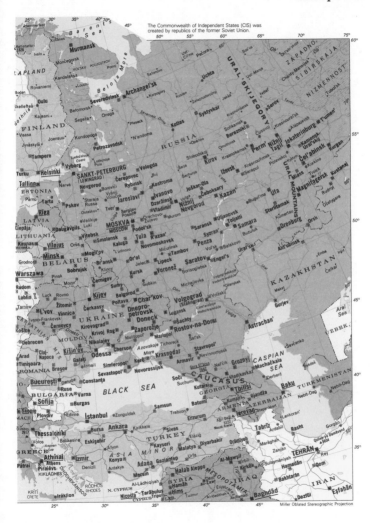

The Commonwealth of Independent States (CIS) was created by republics of the former Soviet Union.

Miller Oblated Stereographic Projection

Conic Projection, Two Standard Parallels

Kilometres 0 50 100 150 Km.
Miles 0 50 100 150 Mi.

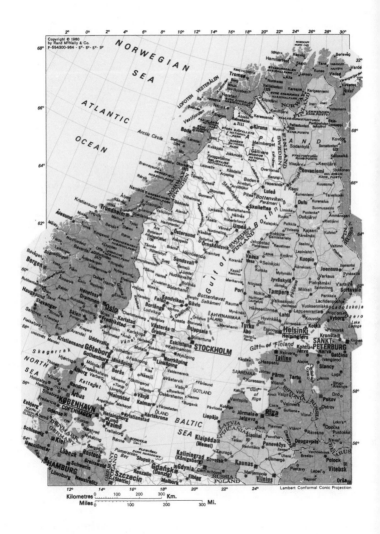

Lambert Conformal Conic Projection

Kilometres 0 | 100 | 200 | 300 Km.
Miles 0 | 100 | 200 | 300 Mi.

8

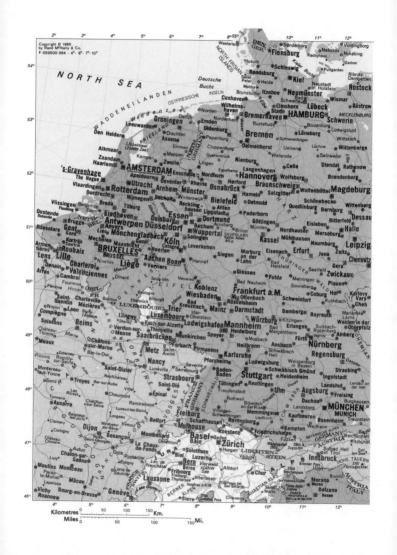

NORTH SEA

Kilometres
Miles

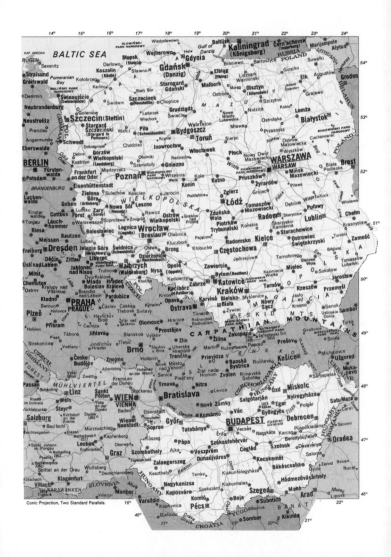

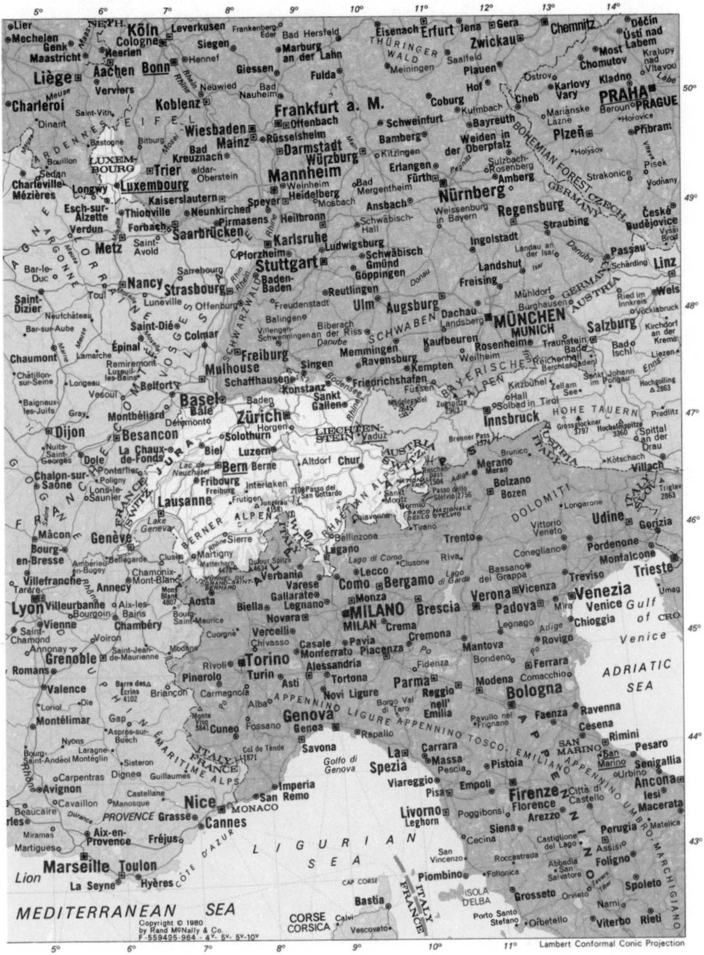
Liège
Maastricht
Köln
Cologne
Leverkusen
Bonn
Aachen
Koblenz
Frankfurt a. M.
Offenbach
Wiesbaden
Mainz
Darmstadt
Würzburg
Mannheim
Heidelberg
Karlsruhe
Stuttgart
Nürnberg
Regensburg
Erfurt
Jena
Gera
Zwickau
Chemnitz
Plauen
Hof
Coburg
Bayreuth
Bamberg
Schweinfurt
Fulda
Giessen
Siegen
Marburg an der Lahn
Bad Hersfeld
THÜRINGER WALD
Meiningen
Cheb
Karlovy Vary
PRAHA
PRAGUE
Plzeň
Strakonice
České Budějovice
BOHEMIAN FOREST
GERMANY
CZECH.
Děčín
Ústí nad Labem
Most
Chomutov
Kladno
Příbram
Písek
Trier
Luxembourg
LUXEMBOURG
Saarbrücken
Kaiserslautern
Neunkirchen
Pirmasens
Speyer
Heilbronn
Ludwigsburg
Schwäbisch Gmünd
Göppingen
Ansbach
Fürth
Erlangen
Amberg
Weiden in der Oberpfalz
Ingolstadt
Straubing
Landshut
Passau
Linz
Freising
Augsburg
Ulm
Reutlingen
MÜNCHEN
MUNICH
Dachau
Kaufbeuren
Rosenheim
Salzburg
Wels
Kempten
Memmingen
Ravensburg
Friedrichshafen
Konstanz
Freiburg
Mulhouse
Basel
Bâle
Zürich
Sankt Gallen
Schaffhausen
Bern
Berne
Luzern
Biel
Solothurn
Fribourg
Interlaken
Chur
LIECHTENSTEIN
Vaduz
Innsbruck
HOHE TAUERN
Villach
Bolzano
Bozen
Merano
Meran
Trento
DOLOMITI
Udine
Gorizia
Trieste
Pordenone
Monfalcone
Treviso
Venezia
Venice
Padova
Vicenza
Verona
Chioggia
Rovigo
Ferrara
Bologna
Modena
Reggio nell' Emilia
Parma
Mantova
Cremona
Brescia
Bergamo
Como
Lecco
Lugano
MILANO
MILAN
Monza
Pavia
Novara
Vercelli
Biella
Torino
Turin
Alessandria
Asti
Cuneo
Genova
Genoa
Savona
Rapallo
Imperia
San Remo
La Spezia
Carrara
Massa
Pistoia
Pisa
Livorno
Leghorn
Firenze
Florence
Arezzo
Siena
Perugia
Assisi
Foligno
Spoleto
Viterbo
Rieti
Grosseto
Piombino
Ravenna
Rimini
SAN MARINO
Pesaro
Ancona
ADRIATIC SEA
Gulf of Venice
LIGURIAN SEA
Golfo di Genova
CORSE
CORSICA
Bastia
Calvi
MEDITERRANEAN SEA
Marseille
Toulon
Nice
MONACO
Cannes
Grasse
Fréjus
Aix-en-Provence
Avignon
PROVENCE
MARITIME ALPS
Gap
Valence
Grenoble
Chambéry
Annecy
Genève
Lausanne
Lake Geneva
BERNER ALPEN
Lyon
Villeurbanne
Vienne
Saint-Étienne
Mâcon
Bourg-en-Bresse
Dijon
Besançon
Belfort
Montbéliard
Colmar
Strasbourg
Nancy
Metz
Épinal
Verdun
Charleroi
Dinant
Sedan
Charleville-Mézières
Chaumont
Chalon-sur-Saône
JURA
VOSGES
LORRAINE
ARGONNE
ARDENNES
EIFEL
SCHWARZWALD
SCHWABEN
BAYERISCHE ALPEN
AUSTRIA
ITALY
SWITZ.
FRANCE
Copyright © 1980 by Rand McNally & Co.
F-559495-964 - 4V- 5V- 5V-10V
Lambert Conformal Conic Projection

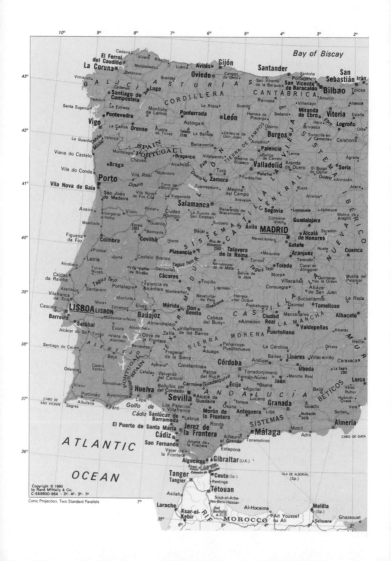

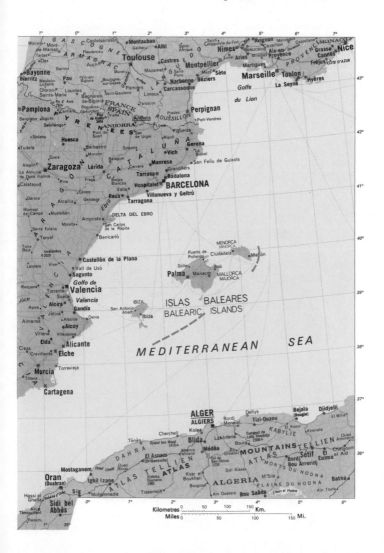

Kilometres 0 50 100 150
Miles 0 50 100 150 Mi.

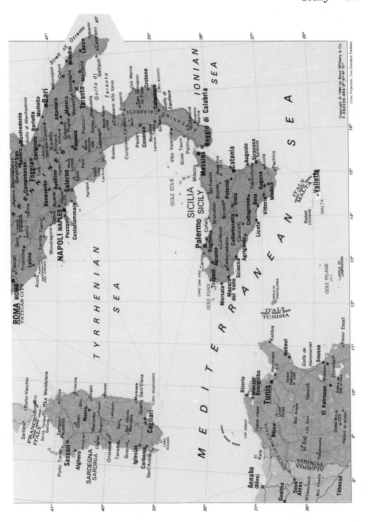

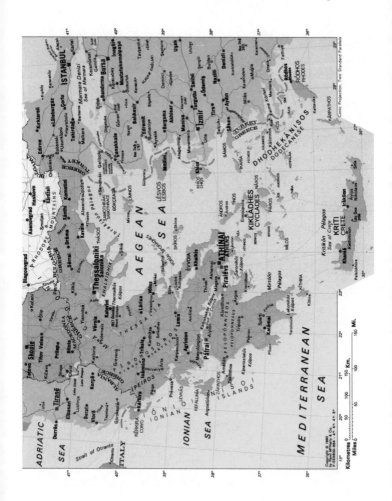

Kilometres 0 200 400 600 Km.

Miles 0 200 400 600 Mi.

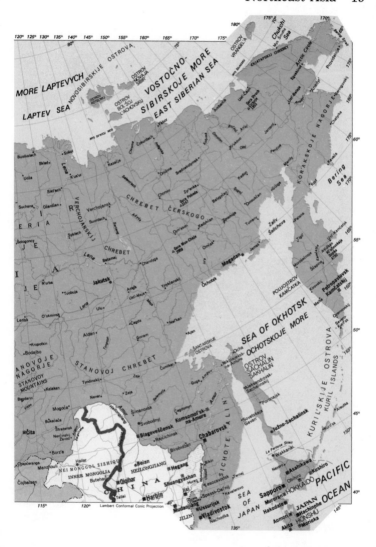

Kilometres 0   200   400   600 Km.

Miles 0   200   400   600 Mi.

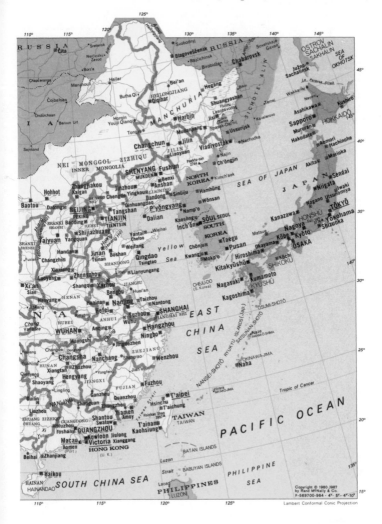

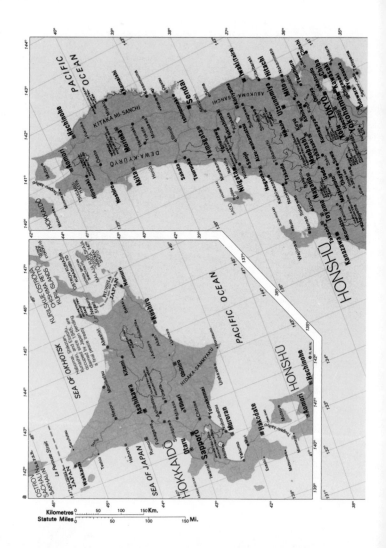

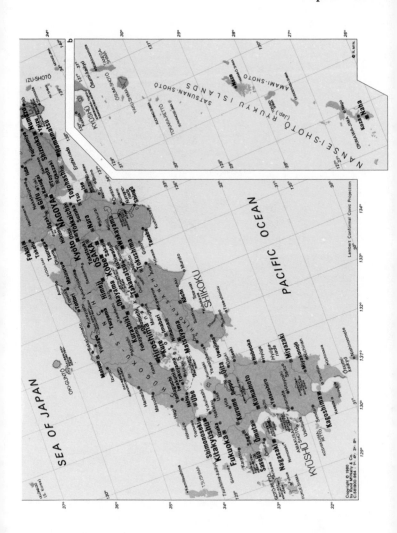

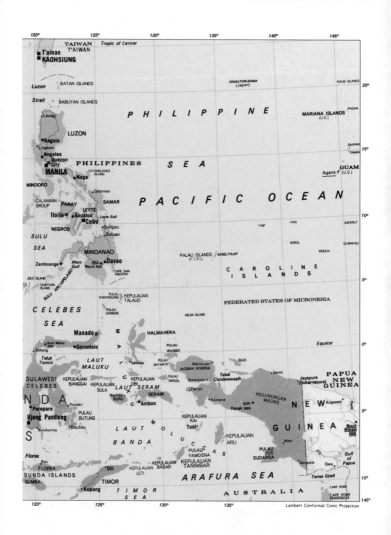

TAIWAN
T'AIWAN
■ T'ainan
■ KAOHSIUNG

Tropic of Cancer

OKINO-TORI-SHIMA
(Japan)

MAUG ISLANDS

20°

Luzon   BATAN ISLANDS

Strait   BABUYAN ISLANDS

PHILIPPINE

MARIANA ISLANDS
(U.S.)

PAGAN

•Laoag

LUZON

SAIPAN
TINIAN

15°

•Baguio
•Lingayen
•Angeles
•Quezon
  City
MANILA   •Naga

PHILIPPINES

CATANDUANES
ISLAND

SEA

Agana ★ (U.S.)

GUAM

MINDORO

•Catarman

CALAMIAN
GROUP   PANAY

SAMAR

PACIFIC   OCEAN

Iloilo■ ■Bacolod
NEGROS   •Cebu

LEYTE
Leyte Gulf

•Surigao

YAP

FAIS

GAFERUT

10°

SULU
SEA

•Butuan

MINDANAO

SOROL

WOLEAI

OLIMARAO

Zamboanga•   Moro
Gulf   2954 ▲Davao
Mount Apô

PALAU ISLANDS
(T.T.P.I.)   BABELTHUAP

CAROLINE

JOLO ISLAND

CAPE SAN
AGUSTIN

ISLANDS

5°

TAWITAWI
ISLAND

SULU ARCHIPELAGO

PULAU
KARAKELONG   KEPULAUAN
TALAUD

FEDERATED STATES OF MICRONESIA

CELEBES
SEA

PULAU
SANGHE

HELEN ISLAND

Manado ⌐

HALMAHERA

Equator

0°

▲Bukit Maline
2443
•Sabang   •Gorontalo

PULAU
WAIGEO

Teluk
Tomini

LAUT
MALUKU

•Labuha

PULAU
BATANTA

PULAU
MISOOL   •Manokwari

JAZIRAH DOBERAI

•BIAK

Teluk
Cenderawasih   •Sarmi

Jayapura
(Sukarnapura)   PAPUA
NEW
GUINEA

SULAWESI
CELEBES   KEPULAUAN
BANGGAI   KEPULAUAN
SULA

LAUT
OBI   SERAM

•Faklok

•Kaimana   PEGUNUNGAN
MAOKE

NEW

•Aingoram

N D A   Namlea
•   BURU
•Parepare   •Kendari

SERAM
•Ambon

5030 ▲
Puncak Jaya

5°

Ujung Pandang
S

PULAU
BUTUNG   KEPULAUAN
KAI
Tual•

GUINEA

Mount
Wilhelm
4509

•Bulukumba   •Baubau

LAUT
BANDA   M
O
L
U
PULAUC
YAMDENA
C
A
S   KEPULAUAN
ARU

PULAU
YOS
SUDARSA   •Mapi

Gulf
of
Papua

Flores
•Reo

KEPULAUAN
TANIMBAR

•Merauke   Danu•

FLORES
SUNDA ISLANDS

•Dili   KEPULAUAN BABAR
LETI   KEPULAUAN   ARAFURA   SEA

Torres Strait

CAPE YORK

SUMBA   TIMOR   •Kupang

TIMOR
SEA   AUSTRALIA

CAPE YORK
PENINSULA

10°

120°   125°   130°   135°   145°

Lambert Conformal Conic Projection

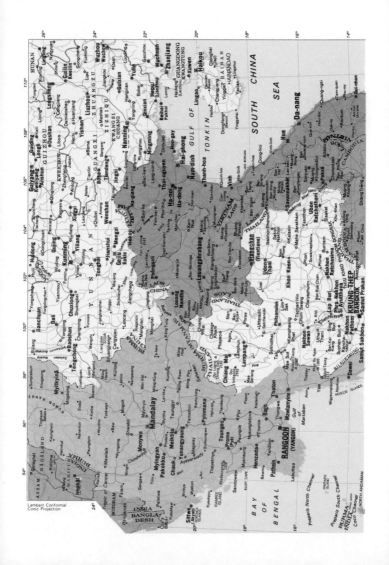

Lambert Conformal
Conic Projection

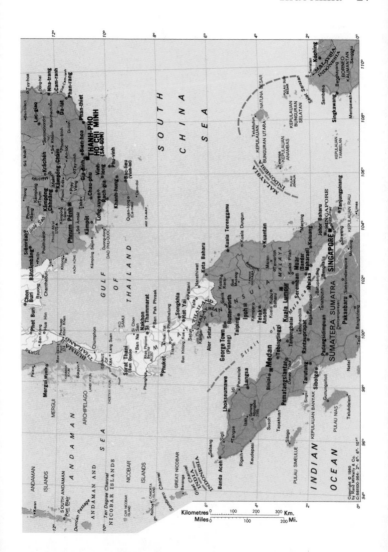

Kilometres 0 100 200 300 Km.
Miles 0 100 200 Mi.

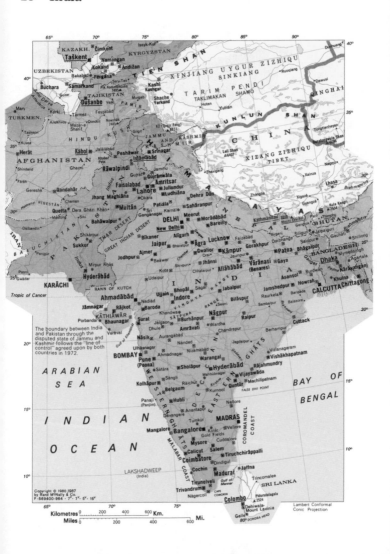

The boundary between India and Pakistan through the disputed state of Jammu and Kashmir follows the "line of control" agreed upon by both countries in 1972.

Copyright © 1980/1987
by Rand McNally & Co.
F-569400-964 - 7° - 7° - 5° - 16°

Lambert Conformal
Conic Projection

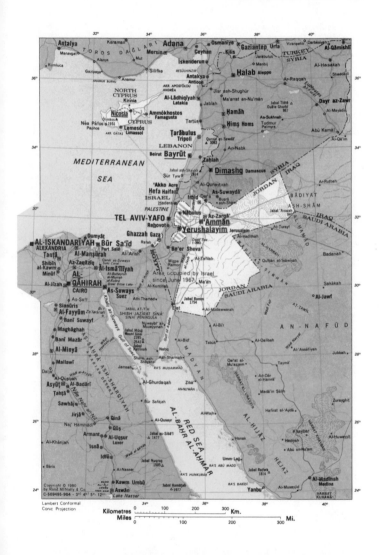

Copyright © 1980
by Rand McNally & Co.
C-669495-964

Lambert Conformal
Conic Projection

Kilometres 0   100   200   300 Km.
Miles 0   100   200   300 Mi.

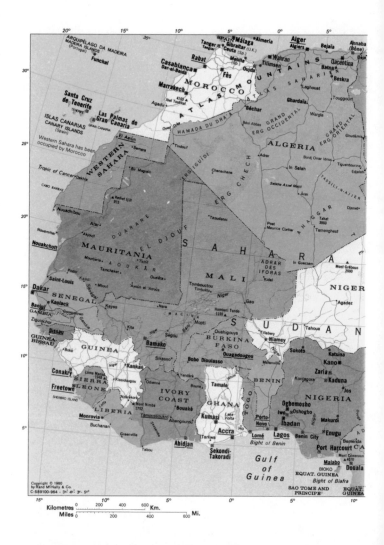

Kilometres 0 200 400 600 Km.

Miles 0 200 400 600 Mi.

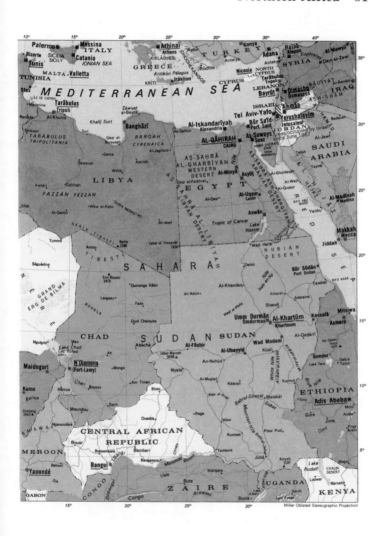

Miller Oblated Stereographic Projection

Kilometres 0 200 400 600 Km.
Miles 0 200 400 600 Mi.

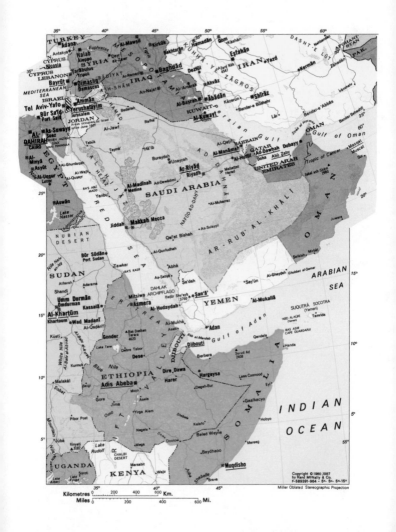

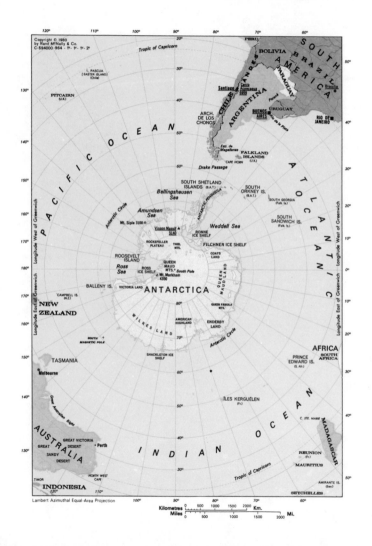

Lambert Azimuthal Equal-Area Projection

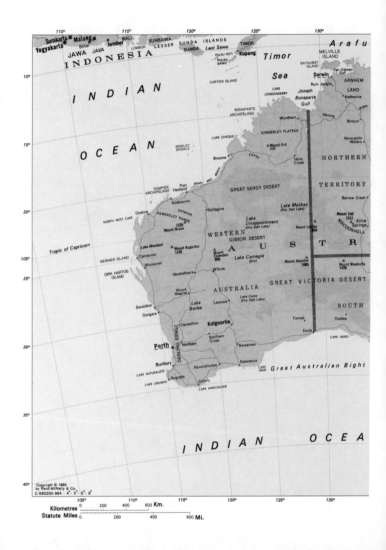

Kilometres 0 200 400 600 Km.

Statute Miles 0 200 400 600 Mi.

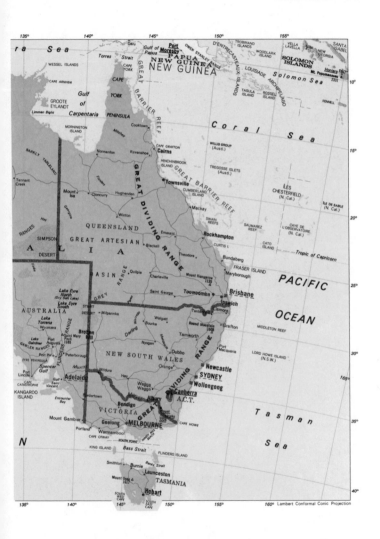

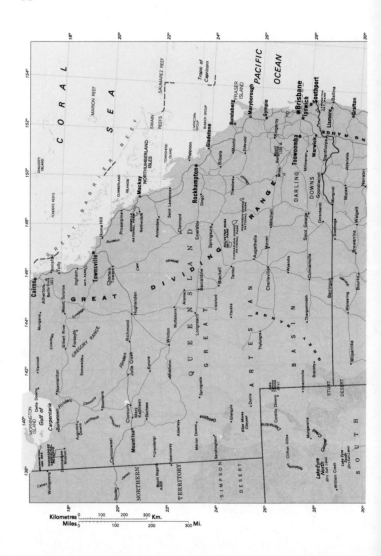

Kilometres 0 | 100 | 200 | 300 Km.
Miles 0 | 100 | 200 | 300 Mi.

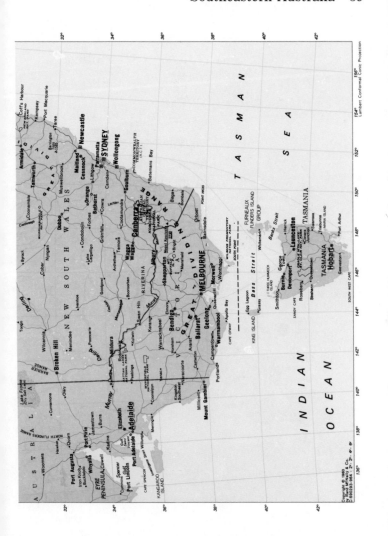

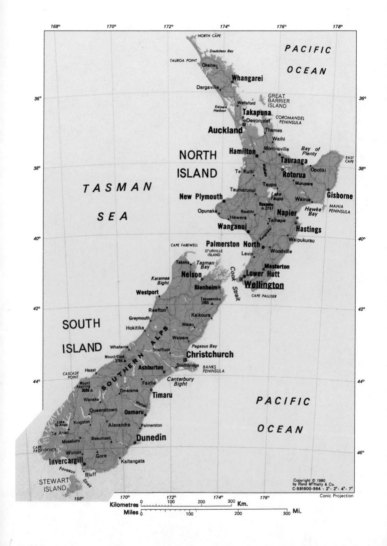

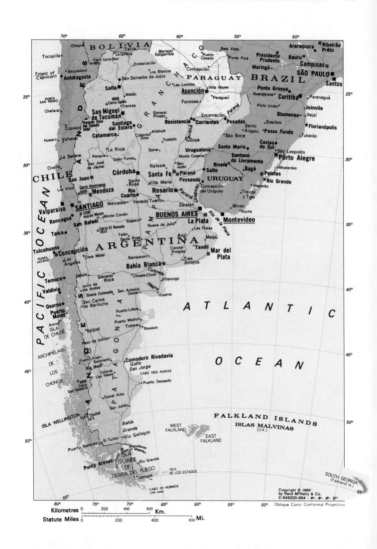

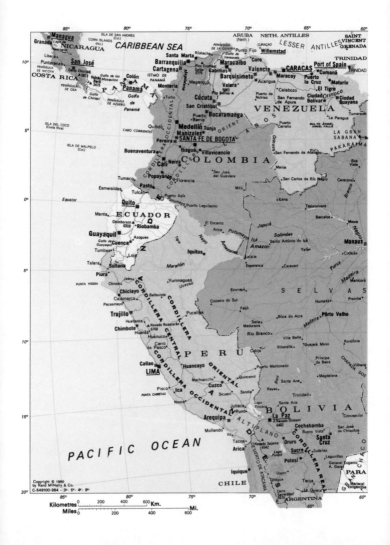

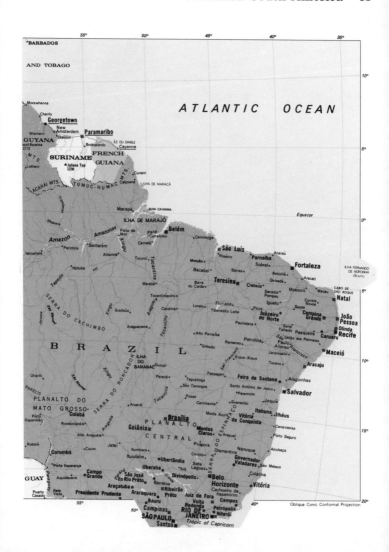

ATLANTIC OCEAN

Morawhanna

Charity
New
Amsterdam
Skeldon

Georgetown

Paramaribo

Wismar
GUYANA

ILE DU DIABLE
Cayenne

Brokopondo

Mt Roraima
2772

SURINAME
FRENCH
GUIANA

Lethem

Juliana Top
1290

Cunani

ACARAI MTS

TUMUC-HUMAC MTS

Calçoene

ILHA DE MARACÁ

Macapá
ILHA CAVIANA

Equator

Manaus

ILHA DE MARAJÓ

Amazon

Amazonas

Porto de
Moz
Curralinho

Belém

Caninde

Pará

São Luís

Rosário

Parnaíba

Acaraú

Camocim

Itacoatiara

Santarém

Parintins

Cametá

Monção

Bacabal

Barras

Sobral

Fortaleza

Quixadá

Altamira

Tucuruí

Teresina

Crateús

Beberibe

Itaituba

Tapajós

Xingu

Iriri

Tocantins

Bom
do Corda

Senador
Pompeu

Moassoro

Macau

Currais
Novos

Natal

CABO DE
SÃO ROQUE

ILHA FERNANDO
DE NORONHA
(Brazil)

Marabá

Tocantinópolis

Floriano

Picos

Iguatu

Sousa

Gradaús

Carolina

Loreto

Benedito Leite

Juàzeiro
do Norte

Campina
Grande

João
Pessoa

SERRA DO CACHIMBO

Araguacema

Alto Parnaíba

Paulistana

Serra
Talhada

Pesqueira

Caruaru

Olinda
Recife

B R A Z I L

Tocantins

Gilbués

Ramanso

Petrolina

São Francisco

União dos Palmares

Maceió

ILHA
DO
BANANAL

Guspi

Xique-Xique

Jeremoabo

Tucano

Aracaju

Utiariti

Paraná

Teguatinga

Passagem

Feira de Santana

Alagoinhas

Santo Antônio de Jesus

Anuará

Posse

São Domingos

Salvador

PARECIS

Tocantins

Carinhanha

Guanambi

Paramirim

Jequié

Itabuna

Ilhéus

PLANALTO DO

MATO GROSSO

Arany

Alto Araguaia

Brasília

PLANALTO

Monte Azul

Vitória da
Conquista

Porto
Esperidião

Cuiabá

Goiânia

Montes
Claros

Araçuaí

Canavieiras

Pôrto Seguro

Rondonópolis

CENTRAL

Pirapora

Diamantina

Nanuque

Roboré

Coxim

Jataí

Itumbiara

Corinto

Governador
Valadares

São Mateus

Corumbá

Pôrto Esperança

Aquidauana

Ituiutaba

Uberlândia

Sete
Lagoas

Colatina

Diamantino

Belo
Horizonte

Vitória

GUAY

Puerto
Casado

Bela
Vista

Campo
Grande

São José
do Rio Prêto

Uberaba

Divinópolis

Cachoeiro de
Itapemirim

Presidente Prudente

Araçatuba

Barretos

Ibiá

Campos

Petrópolis

Araraquara

Bauru

Ribeirão
Prêto

Juiz de Fora

Volta
Redonda

Niterói

Campinas

RIO DE
JANEIRO

SÃO PAULO

Santos

Tropic of Capricorn

Oblique Conic Conformal Projection

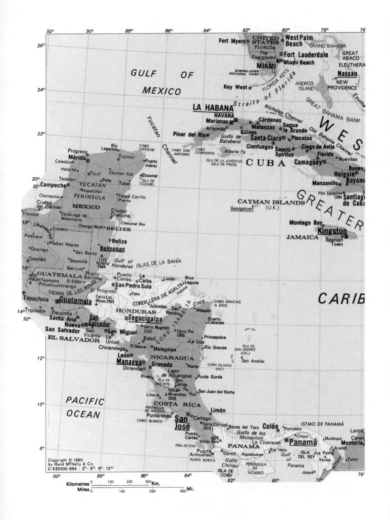

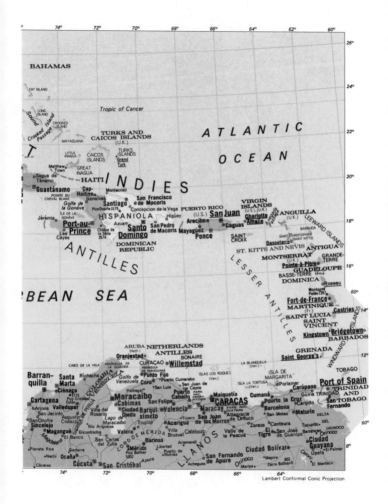

Lambert Conformal Conic Projection

46

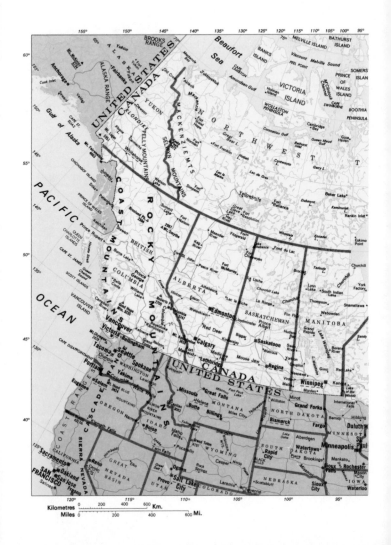

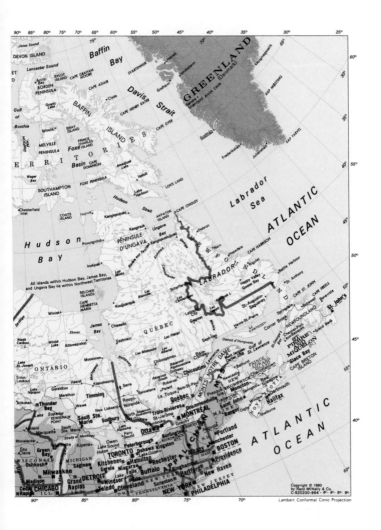

Copyright © 1980
by Rand McNally & Co.
C-520200-964 - 6°- 4°- 6°- 9°

Lambert Conformal Conic Projection

Kilometres 0   200   400   600 Km.

Miles 0   200   400   600 Mi.

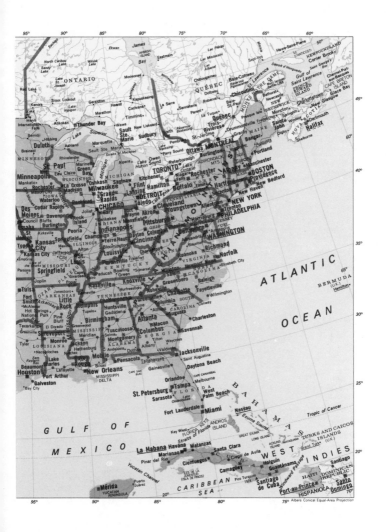

Albers Conical Equal-Area Projection

Kilometres 0 50 100 150 Km.

Miles 0 50 100 150 Mi.

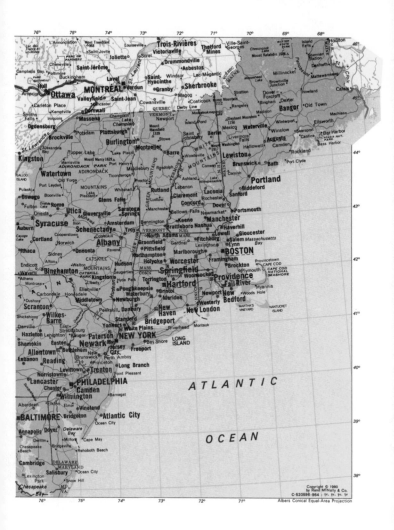

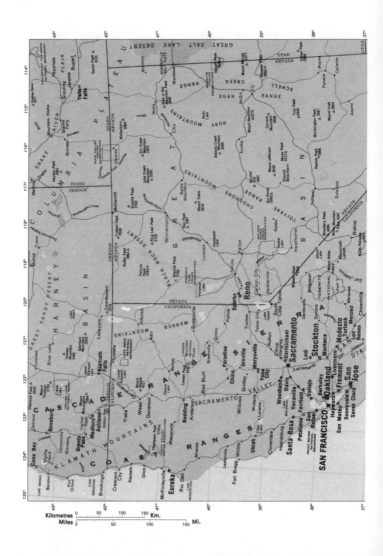

Kilometres 0 50 100 150 Km.

Miles 0 50 100 150 Mi.

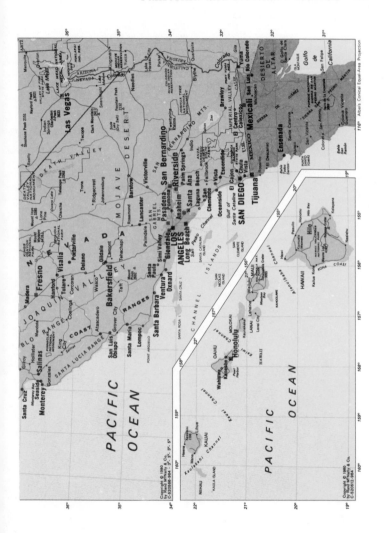

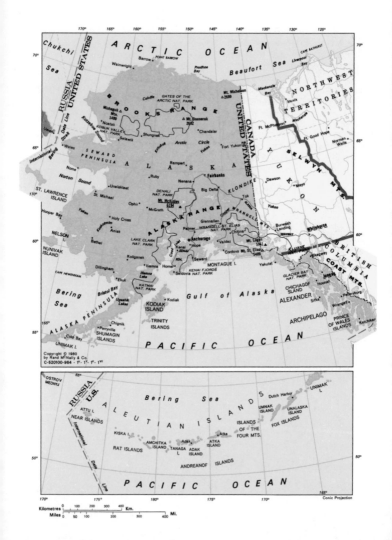

Copyright © 1980
by Rand McNally & Co.
C-520100-964 - 1°- 1°- 1ˢᵗ

Conic Projection

Kilometres
0   100   200   300   400   Km.

Miles
0   50   100   200   300   400   Mi.

INTRODUCTION TO THE INDEX

Local official names are used on the maps and in the index. Features that extend beyond the boundaries of one country and have no single official name are usually named in English. Many conventional English names and former names are cross-referenced to the official names.

The names of physical features may appear inverted, since they are always alphabetized under the proper, not the generic, part of the name, thus: "Gibraltar, Strait of ʊ". Otherwise every entry, whether consisting of one word or more, is alphabetized as a single continuous entity. "La Habana," for example, appears after "Lagos" and before "Lahore." Names beginning with articles (Al-Qāhirah, Ad-Dawhah) are not inverted. Names beginning "St." are alphabetized as though spelled "Saint." Entries that are completely identical (including symbols, discussed below) are distinguished by abbreviations of their official country names. The country abbreviations used for places in the United States, Canada and United Kingdom indicate the state, province or political division in which the feature is located. (See List of Abbreviations below).

City names are not followed by symbols. The names of all other features are followed by symbols that graphically represent kinds of features, for example, ʌ for mountain (Everest, Mount ʌ). A complete list of symbols follows the List of Abbreviations. All cross-references are indicated by the symbol →.

Page references to two-page maps always refer to the left-hand page. If a page contains several maps or insets, a lowercase letter identifies the specific map or inset.

ABBREVIATIONS

Al., U.S.	Alabama	Guy.	Guyana
B.C., Can.	British Columbia	H.K.	Hong Kong
Cay. Is.	Cayman Islands	S.C., U.S.	South Carolina
Eng., U.K.	England	Sey.	Seychelles
		W.V., U.S.	West Virginia

SYMBOLS

ʌ	**Mountain**	±	**Other Topographic Features**	ᖨ	**Other Hydrographic Features**	□³	State, Canton, Republic
ʌ¹	Volcano					□⁴	Province, Region, Oblast
ʌ	**Mountains**			ᖨ¹	Ocean		
ϰ	Pass	±¹	Continent	ᖨ²	Sea	□⁸	Miscellaneous
V	Valley, Canyon	≈	River	□	**Political Unit**	□⁹	Historical
⪢	Cape	ʊ	Strait	□¹	Independent Nation	➡	**Miscellaneous**
⪢¹	Peninsula	c	Bay, Gulf	□²	Dependency	➡¹	Region
I	Island	⊜	Lake, Lakes			➡²	Desert
II	Islands						

Name	Page No.	Lat.	Long.
Brahmaputra (Yaluzangbujiang) ≏	28	24.02N	90.55 E
Brasília	42	15.47S	47.55W
Brazil □¹	42	10.00S	55.00W
Brazzaville	32	4.16S	5.17 E
Bridgetown	44	13.06N	59.37W
British Columbia □⁴	48	54.00N	125.00W
Brunei □¹	24	4.30N	114.40 E
Brussels — Bruxelles	8	50.50N	4.20 E
Bruxelles (Brussel)	8	50.50N	4.20 E
Bucureşti (Bucharest)	16	44.26N	26.06 E
Budapest	8	47.30N	19.05 E
Buenos Aires	41	34.36S	58.27W
Bujumbura	32	3.23S	29.22 E
Bulgaria □¹	4	43.00N	25.00 E
Burkina Faso □¹	30	13.00N	2.00W
Burma (Myanmar) □¹	24	22.00N	98.00 E
Burundi □¹	32	3.15S	30.00 E

C

Name	Page No.	Lat.	Long.
Cairo — Al-Qāhirah	30	30.03N	31.15 E
Calcutta	28	22.34N	88.20 E
Calgary	48	51.03N	114.05W
California □³	50	37.30N	119.30W
California, Golfo de ⊂	46	28.00N	112.00W
Cambodia □¹	24	13.00N	105.00 E
Cameroon □¹	30	6.00N	12.00 E
Canada □¹	48	60.00N	95.00W
Canarias, Islas (Canary Islands) II	30	28.00N	15.30W
Canaveral, Cape ≻	50	28.27N	80.32W
Canberra	36	35.17S	149.08 E
Canton — Guangzhou	20	23.06N	113.16 E
Cape Town (Kaapstad)	32	33.55S	18.22 E
Caracas	42	10.30N	66.56W
Cardiff	6	51.29N	3.13W
Caribbean Sea ⊤²	44	15.00N	73.00W
Carpathian Mountains ⋏	4	48.00N	24.00 E
Carson City	54	39.10N	119.46W
Casablanca (Dar-el-Beida)	30	33.39N	7.35W
Cascade Range ⋏	50	49.00N	120.00W
Caspian Sea ⊤²	4	42.00N	50.30 E
Castries	44	14.01N	61.00W
Caucasus ⋏	4	42.30N	45.00 E
Cayenne	42	4.56N	52.20W
Cayman Islands □²	44	19.30N	80.40W
Cebu	24	10.18N	123.54 E
Celebes — Sulawesi I	24	2.00S	121.00 E
Central African Republic □¹	30	7.00N	21.00 E
Chad □¹	30	15.00N	19.00 E
Chang (Yangtze) ≏	20	31.48N	121.10 E
Char'kov	4	50.00N	36.15 E
Charleston, S.C., U.S.	50	32.46N	79.55W
Charleston, W.V., U.S.	52	38.20N	81.37W
Charlotte Amalie	44	18.21N	64.56W
Charlottetown	48	46.14N	63.08W
Cheyenne	50	41.08N	104.49W
Chicago	50	41.51N	87.39W
Chile □¹	41	30.00S	71.00W
China □¹	20	35.00N	105.00 E
Christchurch	40	43.32S	172.38 E
Cincinnati	52	39.09N	84.27W

Name	Page No.	Lat.	Long.
Ciudad de México (Mexico City)	46	19.24N	99.09W
Ciudad Juárez	46	31.44N	106.29W
Cleveland	52	41.29N	81.41W
Coast Ranges ⋏	50	41.00N	123.30W
Cologne — Köln	8	50.56N	6.59 E
Colombia □¹	42	4.00N	72.00W
Colombo	28	6.56N	79.51 E
Colorado □³	50	39.30N	105.30W
Colorado ≏	50	31.54N	114.57W
Columbia	50	34.00N	81.02W
Columbia ≏	48	46.15N	124.05W
Columbus	52	39.57N	82.59W
Comoros □¹	32	12.10S	44.10 E
Conakry	30	9.31N	13.43W
Concord	52	43.12N	71.32W
Congo □¹	32	1.00S	15.00 E
Congo (Zaïre) ≏	32	6.04S	12.24 E
Connecticut □³	50	41.45N	72.45W
Cook Islands □²	2	20.00S	158.00W
Copenhagen — København	7	55.40N	12.35 E
Coral Sea ⊤²	2	20.00S	158.00 E
Cork	6	51.54N	8.28W
Corse (Corsica) I	14	42.00N	9.00 E
Costa Rica □¹	44	10.00N	84.00W
Crete — Kríti I	16	35.29N	24.42 E
Croatia □¹	14	45.10N	15.30 E
Cuba □¹	44	21.30N	80.00W
Cyprus □¹	29	35.00N	33.00 E
Czechoslovakia □¹	4	49.30N	17.00 E

D

Name	Page No.	Lat.	Long.
Dakar	30	14.40N	17.26W
Dallas	50	32.46N	96.47W
Damascus — Dimashq	29	33.30N	36.18 E
Danube (Donau) (Dunaj) (Duna) ≏	8	45.20N	29.40 E
Dar es Salaam	32	6.48S	39.17 E
Dead Sea ⊘	29	31.30N	35.30 E
Death Valley V	54	36.30N	117.00W
Delaware □³	50	39.10N	75.30W
Denmark □¹	4	56.00N	10.00 E
Denver	50	39.44N	104.59W
Des Moines	50	41.36N	93.36W
Detroit	52	42.20N	83.03W
Dhaka	28	23.43N	90.25 E
Dimashq (Damascus)	29	33.30N	36.18 E
Djibouti □¹	34	11.30N	43.00 E
Doha — Ad-Dawḥah	34	25.17N	51.32 E
Dominica □¹	44	15.30N	61.20W
Dominican Republic □¹	44	19.00N	70.40W
Douglas	6	54.09N	4.28W
Dover, Strait of (Pas de Calais) ̆	10	51.00N	1.30 E
Dresden	8	51.03N	13.44 E
Dublin (Baile Átha Cliath)	6	53.20N	6.15W
Durban	32	29.55S	30.56 E

E

Name	Page No.	Lat.	Long.
Ecuador □¹	42	2.00S	77.30W
Edinburgh	6	55.57N	3.13W
Edmonton	48	53.33N	113.28W
Egypt □¹	30	27.00N	30.00 E

Name	Page No.	Lat.	Long.
Johannesburg	32	26.15 S	28.00 E
Jordan □ [1]	29	31.00 N	36.00 E
Juneau	56	58.20 N	134.27 W

K

Name	Page No.	Lat.	Long.
K2 ∧	28	35.53 N	76.30 E
Kābol	28	34.30 N	69.11 E
Kampala	32	0.19 N	32.25 E
Kansas □ [3]	50	38.45 N	98.15 W
Karāchi	28	24.52 N	67.03 E
Kāthmāndu	28	27.43 N	85.19 E
Kentucky □ [3]	50	37.30 N	85.15 W
Kenya □ [1]	32	1.00 N	38.00 E
Kharkov			
→ Char'kov	4	50.00 N	36.15 E
Khartoum			
→ Al-Khartūm	30	15.36 N	32.32 E
Khyber Pass)(	28	34.05 N	71.10 E
Kigali	32	1.57 S	30.04 E
Kijev	4	50.26 N	30.31 E
Kingston	44	18.00 N	76.48 W
Kingstown	44	13.09 N	61.14 W
Kinshasa (Léopoldville)	32	4.18 S	15.18 E
Kiribati □ [1]	2	4.00 S	175.00 E
København (Copenhagen)	7	55.40 N	12.35 E
Köln (Cologne)	8	50.56 N	6.59 E
Korea, North □ [1]	20	40.00 N	127.00 E
Korea, South □ [1]	20	36.30 N	128.00 E
Kríti I	16	35.29 N	24.42 E
Krung Thep (Bangkok)	26	13.45 N	100.31 E
Kuala Lumpur	26	3.10 N	101.42 E
Kuwait □ [1]	34	29.30 N	47.45 E
Kyrgyzstan □ [1]	28	41.00 N	75.00 E
Kyūshū I	22	33.00 N	131.00 E

L

Name	Page No.	Lat.	Long.
Lagos	30	6.27 N	3.24 E
La Habana (Havana)	44	23.08 N	82.22 W
Lahore	28	31.35 N	74.18 E
Lansing	52	42.43 N	84.33 W
Laos □ [1]	24	18.00 N	105.00 E
La Paz	42	16.30 S	68.09 W
Las Vegas	54	36.10 N	115.08 W
Latvia □ [1]	4	57.00 N	25.00 E
Lebanon □ [1]	29	33.50 N	35.50 E
Leipzig	8	51.19 N	12.20 E
Lena ≃	18	72.25 N	126.40 E
Leningrad			
→ Sankt-Peterburg	4	59.55 N	30.15 E
Lesotho □ [1]	32	29.30 S	28.30 E
Lhasa	20	29.40 N	91.09 E
Liberia □ [1]	30	6.00 N	10.00 W
Libreville	32	0.23 N	9.27 E
Libya □ [1]	30	27.00 N	17.00 E
Liechtenstein □ [1]	4	47.09 N	9.35 E
Lilongwe	32	13.59 S	33.44 E
Lima	42	12.03 S	77.03 W
Lincoln	50	40.48 N	96.40 W
Lisboa (Lisbon)	12	38.43 N	9.08 W
Lithuania □ [1]	4	56.00 N	24.00 E
Little Rock	50	34.44 N	92.17 W
Liverpool	6	53.25 N	2.55 W
Logan, Mount ∧	48	60.34 N	140.24 W
Lomé	30	6.08 N	1.13 E
London	6	51.30 N	0.10 W
Londonderry	6	55.00 N	7.19 W
Los Angeles	54	34.03 N	118.14 W
Louisiana □ [3]	50	31.15 N	92.15 W

Name	Page No.	Lat.	Long.
Louisville	50	38.15 N	85.45 W
Luanda	32	8.48 S	13.14 E
Lusaka	32	15.25 S	28.17 E
Luxembourg □ [1]	4	49.45 N	6.05 E
Luzon I	24	16.00 N	121.00 E
Lyon	10	45.45 N	4.51 E

M

Name	Page No.	Lat.	Long.
Macau □ [2]	20	22.10 N	113.33 E
Macedonia □ [1]	16	41.50 N	22.00 E
Madagascar □ [1]	32	19.00 S	46.00 E
Madison	50	43.04 N	89.24 W
Madras	28	13.04 N	80.16 E
Madrid	12	40.24 N	3.41 W
Magallanes, Estrecho de (Strait of Magellan) ⊻	41	54.00 S	71.00 W
Maine □ [3]	50	45.15 N	69.15 W
Makkah (Mecca)	34	21.27 N	39.49 E
Malabo	30	3.45 N	8.47 E
Malawi □ [1]	32	13.30 S	34.00 E
Malaysia □ [1]	24	2.30 N	112.30 E
Mali □ [1]	30	17.00 N	4.00 W
Malta □ [1]	4	35.50 N	14.35 E
Managua	44	12.09 N	86.17 W
Manchester	6	53.30 N	2.15 W
Mandalay	26	22.00 N	96.05 E
Manila	24	14.35 N	121.00 E
Manitoba □ [4]	48	54.00 N	97.00 W
Maputo (Lourenço Marques)	32	25.58 S	32.35 E
Marseille	10	43.18 N	5.24 E
Martinique □ [2]	44	14.40 N	61.00 W
Maryland □ [3]	50	39.00 N	76.45 W
Masqat (Muscat)	34	23.37 N	58.35 E
Massachusetts □ [3]	50	42.15 N	71.50 W
Matterhorn ∧	10	45.59 N	7.43 E
Mauritania □ [1]	30	20.00 N	12.00 W
Mauritius □ [1]	32	20.17 S	57.33 E
Mayotte □ [2]	32	12.50 S	45.10 E
Mbabane	32	26.18 S	31.06 E
McKinley, Mount ∧	56	63.30 N	151.00 W
Mecca			
→ Makkah	34	21.27 N	39.49 E
Mediterranean Sea ⊽ [2]	2	35.00 N	20.00 E
Mekong ≃	26	10.33 N	105.24 E
Melbourne	36	37.49 S	144.58 E
Memphis	50	35.08 N	90.02 W
Mexico □ [1]	46	23.00 N	102.00 W
Mexico, Gulf of ⊂	46	24.00 N	93.00 W
Mexico City			
→ Ciudad de México	46	19.24 N	99.09 W
Miami	50	25.46 N	80.11 W
Michigan □ [3]	50	44.00 N	85.00 W
Michigan, Lake ⊜	50	44.00 N	87.00 W
Micronesia, Federated States of □ [1]	24	5.00 N	152.00 E
Milano (Milan)	14	45.28 N	9.12 E
Milwaukee	50	43.02 N	87.54 W
Mindanao I	24	8.00 N	125.00 E
Minneapolis	50	44.58 N	93.15 W
Minnesota □ [3]	50	46.00 N	94.15 W
Mississippi □ [3]	50	32.50 N	89.30 W
Mississippi ≃	50	29.00 N	89.15 W
Missouri □ [3]	50	38.30 N	93.30 W
Missouri ≃	50	38.50 N	90.08 W
Moldova □ [1]	4	47.00 N	29.00 E
Monaco □ [1]	4	43.45 N	7.25 E
Mongolia □ [1]	20	46.00 N	105.00 E

Name	Page No.	Lat.	Long.
Monrovia	30	6.18 N	10.47 W
Montana □³	50	47.00 N	110.00 W
Montenegro □³	16	42.30 N	19.20 E
Monterrey	46	25.40 N	100.19 W
Montevideo	41	34.53 S	56.11 W
Montgomery	50	32.23 N	86.18 W
Montpelier	52	44.15 N	72.34 W
Montréal	52	45.31 N	73.34 W
Montserrat □²	44	16.45 N	62.12 W
Morocco □¹	30	32.00 N	5.00 W
Moroni	32	11.41 S	43.16 E
Moskva (Moscow)	4	55.45 N	37.35 E
Mozambique □¹	32	18.15 S	35.00 E
München (Munich)	8	48.08 N	11.34 E
Muqdisho	34	2.01 N	45.20 E
Murmansk	4	68.58 N	33.05 E
Muscat → Masqaṭ	34	23.37 N	58.35 E

N

Name	Page No.	Lat.	Long.
Nagoya	22	35.10 N	136.55 E
Nairobi	32	1.17 S	36.49 E
Namibia □¹	32	22.00 S	17.00 E
Nanjing (Nanking)	20	32.03 N	118.47 E
Napoli (Naples)	14	40.51 N	14.17 E
Nashville	50	36.09 N	86.47 W
Nassau	44	25.05 N	77.21 W
N'Djamena (Fort-Lamy)	30	12.07 N	15.03 E
Nebraska □³	50	41.30 N	100.00 W
Nepal □¹	28	28.00 N	84.00 E
Netherlands □¹	4	52.15 N	5.30 E
Netherlands Antilles □²	44	12.15 N	69.00 W
Nevada □³	50	39.00 N	117.00 W
Newark	52	40.44 N	74.10 W
New Brunswick □⁴	48	46.30 N	66.15 W
New Delhi	28	28.36 N	77.15 E
Newfoundland □⁴	48	52.00 N	56.00 W
New Guinea I	24	5.00 S	140.00 E
New Hampshire □³	50	43.35 N	71.40 W
New Jersey □³	50	40.15 N	74.30 W
New Mexico □³	50	34.30 N	106.00 W
New Orleans	50	29.57 N	90.04 W
New York	52	40.43 N	74.01 W
New York □³	50	43.00 N	75.00 W
New Zealand □¹	40	41.00 S	174.00 E
Niamey	30	13.31 N	2.07 E
Nicaragua □¹	44	13.00 N	85.00 W
Nice	10	43.42 N	7.15 E
Nicosia	29	35.10 N	33.22 E
Niger □¹	30	16.00 N	8.00 E
Niger ≃	30	5.33 N	6.33 E
Nigeria □¹	30	10.00 N	8.00 E
Nile (Nahr an-Nīl) ≃	30	30.10 N	31.06 E
Nižnij Novgorod	4	56.20 N	44.00 E
Norfolk	50	36.50 N	76.17 W
Normandie □⁹	10	49.00 N	0.05 W
North America ♣¹	2	45.00 N	100.00 W
North Carolina □³	50	35.30 N	80.00 W
North Dakota □³	50	47.30 N	100.15 W
Northern Ireland □⁸	6	54.40 N	6.45 W
North Sea ₸²	4	55.20 N	3.00 E
Northwest Territories □⁴	48	70.00 N	100.00 W
Norway □¹	4	62.00 N	10.00 E
Nouakchott	30	18.06 N	15.57 W
Novaja Zeml'a II	18	74.00 N	57.00 E
Nova Scotia □⁴	48	45.00 N	63.00 W
Novosibirsk	18	55.02 N	82.55 E

Name	Page No.	Lat.	Long.
Nürnberg	8	49.27 N	11.04 E

O

Name	Page No.	Lat.	Long.
Oahu I	55a	21.30 N	158.00 W
Oder (Odra) ≃	8	53.32 N	14.38 E
Ohio □³	50	40.15 N	82.45 W
Ohio ≃	50	36.59 N	89.08 W
Oklahoma □³	50	35.30 N	98.00 W
Oklahoma City	50	35.28 N	97.30 W
Olympia	50	47.02 N	122.53 W
Omaha	50	41.15 N	95.56 W
Oman □¹	34	22.00 N	58.00 E
Ontario □⁴	48	51.00 N	85.00 W
Ontario, Lake ⊜	50	43.45 N	78.00 W
Oregon □³	50	44.00 N	121.00 W
Orinoco ≃	42	8.37 N	62.15 W
Orkney Islands II	6	59.00 N	3.00 W
Ōsaka	22	34.40 N	135.30 E
Oslo	7	59.55 N	10.45 E
Ottawa	52	45.25 N	75.42 W
Ouagadougou	30	12.22 N	1.31 W

P

Name	Page No.	Lat.	Long.
Pacific Ocean ₸¹	2	10.00 S	150.00 W
Pakistan □¹	28	30.00 N	70.00 E
Palermo	14	38.07 N	13.21 E
Palestine □⁹	29	32.00 N	35.15 E
Panamá	44	8.58 N	79.32 W
Panama □¹	44	9.00 N	80.00 W
Papua New Guinea □¹	6	6.00 S	143.00 E
Paraguay □¹	41	23.00 S	58.00 W
Paramaribo	42	5.50 N	55.10 W
Paris	10	48.52 N	2.20 E
Peking → Beijing	20	39.55 N	116.25 E
Pennsylvania □³	50	40.45 N	77.30 W
Persian Gulf c	34	27.00 N	51.00 E
Peru □¹	42	10.00 S	76.00 W
Philadelphia	52	39.57 N	75.09 W
Philippines □¹	24	13.00 N	122.00 E
Phnum Pénh	26	11.33 N	104.55 E
Phoenix	50	33.26 N	112.04 W
Pierre	50	44.22 N	100.21 W
Pikes Peak ʌ	50	38.51 N	105.03 W
Pittsburgh	52	40.26 N	79.59 W
Pointe-à-Pitre	44	16.14 N	61.32 W
Poland □¹	4	52.00 N	19.00 E
Port-au-Prince	44	18.32 N	72.20 W
Portland	50	45.31 N	122.40 W
Port Louis	32	20.10 S	57.30 E
Port Moresby	36	9.30 S	147.10 E
Porto	12	41.11 N	8.36 W
Port of Spain	44	10.39 N	61.31 W
Porto-Novo	30	6.29 N	2.37 E
Portugal □¹	4	39.30 N	8.00 W
Poznań	8	52.25 N	16.55 E
Prague → Praha	8	50.05 N	14.26 E
Praha (Prague)	8	50.05 N	14.26 E
Pretoria	32	25.45 S	28.10 E
Prince Edward Island □⁴	48	46.20 N	63.20 W
Providence	52	41.49 N	71.24 W
Puerto Rico □²	44	18.15 N	66.30 W
Pusan	20	35.06 N	129.03 E
P'yŏngyang	20	39.01 N	125.45 E

Name	Page No.	Lat.	Long.
Pyrenees ⋏	12	42.40N	1.00 E
Q			
Qatar □¹	34	25.00N	51.10 E
Quebec (Québec) □⁴	48	52.00N	72.00W
Quito	42	0.13S	78.30W
R			
Rabat	30	34.02N	6.51W
Raleigh	50	35.46N	78.38W
Rangoon (Yangon)	26	16.47N	96.10 E
Red Sea ≂²	34	20.00N	38.00 E
Regina	48	50.25N	104.39W
Reunion □²	32	21.06S	55.36 E
Reykjavik	4	64.09N	21.51W
Rhine (Rhein) (Rhin) □	8	51.52N	6.02 E
Rhode Island □³	50	41.40N	71.30W
Rhodes			
— Ródhos I	16	36.10N	28.00 E
Richmond	50	37.33N	77.27W
Rio de Janeiro	42	22.54S	43.14W
Riyadh			
— Ar-Riyāḍ	34	24.38N	46.43 E
Rocky Mountains ⋏	2	48.00N	116.00W
Ródhos I	16	36.10N	28.00 E
Roma (Rome)	14	41.54N	12.29 E
Romania □¹	4	46.00N	25.30 E
Roseau	44	15.18N	61.24W
Rotterdam	8	51.55N	4.28 E
Russia □¹	2	60.00N	100.00 E
Rwanda □¹	32	2.30S	30.00 E
S			
Sachalin, Ostrov (Sakhalin) I	18	51.00N	143.00 E
Sacramento	54	38.34N	121.29W
Sahara ⬳²	30	26.00N	13.00 E
Sai-gon			
— Thanh-pho Ho Chi Minh	26	10.45N	106.40 E
Saint-Denis	32	20.52S	55.28 E
Saint George's	44	12.03N	61.45W
Saint Helier	10	49.12N	2.37W
Saint John	48	45.16N	66.03W
Saint John's	48	47.34N	52.43W
Saint Kitts and Nevis □¹	44	17.20N	62.45W
Saint Lawrence ≤	48	49.30N	67.00W
Saint Louis	50	38.37N	90.11W
Saint Lucia □¹	44	13.53N	60.58W
Saint Paul	50	44.57N	93.05W
Saint Peter Port	10	49.27N	2.32W
Saint Petersburg			
— Sankt-Peterburg	4	59.55N	30.15 E
Saint Pierre and Miquelon □²	48	46.55N	56.10W
Saint Vincent and the Grenadines □¹	44	13.15N	61.12W
Salem	50	44.56N	123.02W
Salt Lake City	50	40.45N	111.53W
Samara	4	53.12N	50.09 E
San'ā'	34	15.23N	44.12 E
San Antonio	50	29.25N	98.29W
San Diego	54	32.42N	117.09W
San Francisco	54	37.46N	122.25W
San José	44	9.56N	84.05W
San Juan	44	18.28N	66.07W
Sankt-Peterburg	4	59.55N	30.15 E
San Marino □¹	14	43.56N	12.25 E

Name	Page No.	Lat.	Long.
San Salvador	44	13.41N	89.17W
Santa Fe de Bogotá	42	4.36N	74.05W
Santiago	41	33.27S	70.40W
Santo Domingo	44	18.28N	69.54W
São Francisco ≤	42	10.30S	36.24W
São Paulo	42	23.32S	46.37W
Sao Tome and Principe □¹	32	1.00N	7.00 E
Sapporo	22a	43.03N	141.21 E
Sarajevo	16	43.52N	18.25 E
Sardegna (Sardinia) I	14	40.00N	9.00 E
Saskatchewan □⁴	48	54.00N	105.00W
Saudi Arabia □¹	34	25.00N	45.00 E
Scotland □⁸	6	57.00N	4.00W
Seattle	50	47.36N	122.19W
Senegal □¹	30	14.00N	14.00W
Seoul			
— Sŏul	20	37.33N	126.58 E
Serbia □³	16	44.00N	21.00 E
Sevilla	12	37.23N	5.59W
Seychelles □¹	32	4.35S	55.40 E
's-Gravenhage (The Hague)	8	52.06N	4.18 E
Shanghai	20	31.14N	121.28 E
Shenyang	20	41.48N	123.27 E
Shetland Islands II	6	60.30N	1.30W
Sibir' (Siberia) ⬳¹	18	65.00N	110.00 E
Sicilia (Sicily) I	14	37.30N	14.00 E
Sierra Leone □¹	30	8.30N	11.30W
Singapore □¹	24	1.22N	103.48 E
Slovenia □¹	14	46.15N	15.10 E
Snake ≤	50	46.12N	119.02W
Sofija (Sofia)	16	42.41N	23.19 E
Solomon Islands □¹	2	8.00S	159.00 E
Somalia □¹	34	10.00N	49.00 E
Sŏul (Seoul)	20	37.33N	126.58 E
South Africa □¹	32	30.00S	26.00 E
South America ⋏¹	2	15.00S	60.00W
South Carolina □³	50	34.00N	81.00W
South Dakota □³	50	44.15N	100.00W
Spain □¹	4	40.00N	4.00W
Springfield	50	39.48N	89.38W
Sri Lanka □¹	28	7.00N	81.00 E
Stalingrad			
— Volgograd	4	48.44N	44.25 E
Stockholm	7	59.20N	18.03 E
Stuttgart	8	48.46N	9.11 E
Sudan □¹	30	15.00N	30.00 E
Sulawesi (Celebes) I	24	2.00S	121.00 E
Sumatera (Sumatra) I	24	0.05S	102.00 E
Superior, Lake ⊜	50	48.00N	88.00W
Surabaya	24	7.15S	112.45 E
Suriname □¹	42	4.00N	56.00W
Swaziland □¹	32	26.30S	31.30 E
Sweden □¹	4	62.00N	15.00 E
Switzerland □¹	4	47.00N	8.00 E
Sydney	36	33.52S	151.13 E
Syria □¹	29	35.00N	38.00 E
T			
T'aipei	20	25.03N	121.30 E
Taiwan □¹	20	23.30N	121.00 E
Tajikistan □¹	28	39.00N	71.00 E
Taklimakan Shamo ⬳²	20	39.00N	83.00 E
Tallahassee	50	30.26N	84.16W
Tanzania □¹	32	6.00S	35.00 E
Tarābulus (Tripoli)	30	32.54N	13.11 E
Taškent	28	41.20N	69.18 E
Tasmania □³	36	43.00S	147.00 E

Name	Page No.	Lat.	Long.
Tegucigalpa	44	14.06N	87.13W
Tehrān	4	35.40N	51.26 E
Tel Aviv-Yafo	29	32.04N	34.46 E
Tennessee □³	50	35.50N	85.30W
Texas □³	50	31.30N	99.00W
Thailand □¹	24	15.00N	100.00 E
Thames ≏	6	51.28N	0.43 E
Thanh-pho Ho Chi Minh (Sai-gon)	26	10.45N	106.40 E
The Hague → 's-Gravenhage	8	52.06N	4.18 E
Thimphu	20	27.28N	89.39 E
Tigris (Dijlah) ≏	34	31.00N	47.25 E
Tijuana	46	32.32N	117.01W
Tirana	16	41.20N	19.50 E
Titicaca, Lago ◎	42	15.50S	69.20W
Togo □¹	30	8.00N	1.10 E
Tōkyō	22	35.42N	139.46 E
Tonga □¹	2	20.00S	175.00W
Tonkin, Gulf of c	26	20.00N	108.00 E
Topeka	50	39.02N	95.40W
Toronto	48	43.39N	79.23W
Trenton	50	40.13N	74.44W
Trinidad and Tobago □¹	44	11.00N	61.00W
Tripoli → Tarābulus	30	32.54N	13.11 E
Tucson	50	32.13N	110.55W
Tulsa	50	36.09N	95.59W
Tunis	30	36.48N	10.11 E
Tunisia □¹	30	34.00N	9.00 E
Turkey □¹	4	39.00N	35.00 E
Turkmenistan □¹	2	40.00N	60.00 E
Turks and Caicos Islands □²	44	21.45N	71.35W

U

Name	Page No.	Lat.	Long.
Uganda □¹	32	1.00N	32.00 E
Ukraine □¹	4	49.00N	32.00 E
Ulaanbaatar	20	47.55N	106.53 E
Ulan Bator → Ulaanbaatar	20	47.55N	106.53 E
United Arab Emirates □¹	34	24.00N	54.00 E
United Kingdom □¹	4	54.00N	2.00W
United States □¹	50	38.00N	97.00W
Ural'skije Gory ⋌	18	66.00N	63.00 E
Uruguay □¹	41	33.00S	56.00W
Utah □³	50	39.30N	111.30W
Uzbekistan □¹	2	41.00N	64.00 E

V

Name	Page No.	Lat.	Long.
Vaduz	10	47.09N	9.31 E
Valencia	12	39.28N	0.22W
Valletta	14	35.54N	14.31 E
Vancouver	48	49.16N	123.07W
Vatican City (Città del Vaticano) □¹	14	41.54N	12.27 E
Venezia (Venice)	14	45.27N	12.21 E
Venezuela □¹	42	8.00N	66.00W
Veracruz [Llave]	46	19.12N	96.08W
Vermont □³	50	43.50N	72.45W
Vesuvio ⋀¹	14	40.49N	14.26 E

Name	Page No.	Lat.	Long.
Viangchan (Vientiane)	26	17.58N	102.36 E
Victoria, B.C., Can.	48	48.25N	123.22W
Victoria, H.K.	20	22.17N	114.09 E
Victoria, Sey.	32	4.38S	55.27 E
Victoria, Lake ◎	32	1.00S	33.00 E
Vienna → Wien	8	48.13N	16.20 E
Vientiane → Viangchan	26	17.58N	102.36 E
Vietnam □¹	24	16.00N	108.00 E
Virginia □³	50	37.30N	78.45W
Virgin Islands □²	44	18.20N	64.50W
Vladivostok	18	43.10N	131.56 E
Volga ≏	4	45.55N	47.52 E
Volgograd (Stalingrad)	4	48.44N	44.25 E

W

Name	Page No.	Lat.	Long.
Wales □⁸	6	52.30N	3.30W
Warszawa (Warsaw)	8	52.15N	21.00 E
Washington	52	38.53N	77.02W
Washington □³	50	47.30N	120.30W
Wellington	40	41.18S	174.47 E
Western Sahara □²	30	24.30N	13.00W
West Indies ıı	44	19.00N	70.00W
West Virginia □³	50	38.45N	80.30W
Whitehorse	48	60.43N	135.03W
Whitney, Mount ⋀	54	36.35N	118.18W
Wien (Vienna)	8	48.13N	16.20 E
Willemstad	44	12.06N	68.56W
Wilmington	52	39.44N	75.32W
Windhoek	32	22.34S	17.06 E
Winnipeg	48	49.53N	97.09W
Wisconsin □³	50	44.45N	89.30W
Wuhan	20	30.36N	114.17 E
Wyoming □³	50	43.00N	107.30W

Y

Name	Page No.	Lat.	Long.
Yangtze → Chang ≏	20	31.48N	121.10 E
Yaoundé	30	3.52N	11.31 E
Yellow → Huang ≏	20	37.32N	118.19 E
Yellowknife	48	62.27N	114.21W
Yemen □¹	34	15.00N	47.00 E
Yerushalayim (Jerusalem)	29	31.46N	35.14 E
Yokohama	22	35.27N	139.39 E
Yucatan Peninsula ⊁¹	46	19.30N	89.00W
Yugoslavia □¹	4	44.00N	20.00 E
Yukon □⁴	56	64.00N	135.00W
Yukon ≏	56	62.33N	163.59W

Z

Name	Page No.	Lat.	Long.
Zagreb	14	45.48N	15.58 E
Zaire □¹	32	4.00S	25.00 E
Zambezi (Zambeze) ≏	32	18.55S	36.04 E
Zambia □¹	32	15.00S	30.00 E
Zanzibar Island ı	32	6.10S	39.20 E
Zimbabwe □¹	32	20.00S	30.00 E
Zürich	10	47.23N	8.32E